POETRY NOW

NORTH EAST 1996

Edited by Andrew Head

First published in Great Britain in 1996 by
POETRY NOW
1-2 Wainman Road, Woodston,
Peterborough, PE2 7BU

All Rights Reserved

Copyright Contributors 1995

HB ISBN 1 85731 604 5
SB ISBN 1 85731 603 7

FOREWORD

Although we are a nation of poetry writers we are accused of not reading poetry and not buying poetry books: after many years of listening to the incessant gripes of poetry publishers, I can only assume that the books they publish, in general, are books that most people do not want to read.

Poetry should not be obscure, introverted, and as cryptic as a crossword puzzle: it is the poet's duty to reach out and embrace the world.

The world owes the poet nothing and we should not be expected to dig and delve into a rambling discourse searching for some inner meaning.

The reason we write poetry (and almost all of us do) is because we want to communicate: an ideal; an idea; or a specific feeling. Poetry is as essential in communication, as a letter; a radio; a telephone, and the main criteria for selecting the poems in this anthology is very simple: they communicate.

Faced with hundreds of poems and a limited amount of space, the task of choosing the final poems was difficult and as editor one tries to be as detached as possible (quite often editors can become a barrier in the writer-reader exchange) acting as go between, making the connection, not censoring because of personal taste.

In this anthology over one hundred and forty poems are presented to the reader for their enjoyment.

The poetry is written on all levels; the simple and the complex both having their own appeal.

The success of this collection, and all previous *Poetry Now* anthologies, relies on the fact that there are as many individual readers as there are writers, and in the diversity of styles and forms there really is something to please, excite, and hopefully, inspire everyone who reads the book.

CONTENTS

Title	Author	Page
The Last Remaining Dream	Simon Downs	1
On A Lonely Moor	Brian Ducker	2
The Constant Star	Robina Potter	3
The Miner's Eternal Glow	June Stainsby	4
Cut And Dash	Sylvia Gargett	5
Blue For You	J Pounder	6
Legacy Of The Tall Ships	Ruth Henderson	7
Canny Shields	Henry T Harris	8
A Time To Waste	C M Nicholas	10
The Prelude And Conclusion to Love	Lisa McNee	11
Sailors Wear White Ribbons	Creative Writing Group	12
World	Karen Manning	13
John Doe	Elaine Jobson	14
You Are Now	Liz Dinsdale	15
A Mother's Aspirations	S L Johnston	16
Captive Thoughts	Ian Richardson	17
Sea Folk	Josie Brink-Jones	18
The Other Side Of War	Albert Shepherd	19
The Miner	W Harmon	20
God's Heroes	Sean O'Halon	21
Why?	John Robert Ingram	22
Remembrance	Rachel Oxtoby	23
Our Blue-Eyed Lucky	E Pickthall	24
Visions	Jean Cumbor	25
A Residence On The Walk To Causey Arch Beauty Spot	Mary Wright	26
	Heather L Young	27
Peace In The End	Esther Wilson	28
Tobruk 1941	G T Vincent	29
For A Moment	Jackie Pass	31
Down The Pit	K Riley	33
The Alarm Clock	Marjorie Edgar	34
Pride 1995	Damien Whiter	35
The Stars At Night	Ann Watson	36

Nothing Changes	C A Lewis	37
Before The Spartans Came To Blyth	E Barnett	38
My Secret Place	Sylvia Sinclair	39
Ignorance 2000	G Burton	40
A Prayer For Glenn	Carol Renneberg	41
Snapshot Memories Of My Mother	Doreen Dean	42
Birds Of A Feather	Elsie Scrowther	43
A Father	K S Pringle	44
They Knew Not Why	Kenneth Storey	45
Just An Old Heap	Sylvia Rook	46
The Child Who Is Born Today	Sarah Atkin	47
The Best Things In Life Are Free	Norman Guthrie	48
Pallion Can Work	David Reynoldson	49
Fire	Katie O'Brien	50
The Cardboard Hotel	Stephen Wainwright Brown	51
The Poem I Couldn't Write	Laura Graham	52
To My Girlfriend	Michael Griffith	53
Memories	Agnes Summerbell	54
Ode To A Dead Love	Zoe Grant	55
The Escape	Gillian Heron	56
Peace	Jude Ratcliffe	57
North Landing	Ron Marriott	59
Indian Summer	Margery Baston	60
Searching For Nabokov	Tanya Winter	61
Thoughts Of A Redundant Signalman	J Alcock	62
Treasure	G Williams	63
Dilemma	John Mears	64
How Does She Feel	Trudy Appleby	65
Keep Smilin' Through	Bernard M Jackson	66
The Poet And The Lecturer	Joan Peebles	67
Saint Bede's	S A Shippen	68
Wallsend Cranes	Georgina Francis McKellar	69
Age Concern	Pauline Hearnden	70

Market Research Poem	Graham C Brown	71
The Pop Group	Denny Boyce	72
Freeway?	Vera Sykes	73
Untitled	Carol Cobbledick	74
Non-Express, OK!	Tracey Taylor	75
Under The Surface	Andrew Curran	76
Look And Listen	J Facchini	77
Small Potatoes	Jo Colley	78
This Is My Life	Margaret Atkinson	79
My Dad	Lucy Hindmarch	80
Cloud Of Tears	Jane Webber	81
Dad	Carolyn Foggin	82
The Moth Maiden	Joanna Ashwell	83
Meaning And Interpretation II	Aidan Moesby	84
It's In The Bag	Carolyn Brookes	85
Unsolved Crime	Mary Shiells	86
Hearts And Minds	Crystal Indiankhana Candy	87
A Day Out	Olive Cartwright	88
Beatles For Sale - Again!	Ken Jackson	89
Watching Tom Playing The Piano	Robert Mills	90
Once In A While	Jean Cumbor	91
The Candle Flame	Paul Sanders	92
A Moving Story	Tim Butler	93
Voyage To The Stars	Sara Newby	94
Painting	Joy Scarr	95
The Man	Bernard Harry Reay	96
Dreams	M Hulse	97
The Reaper's Tales	Peter Lennox	98
Through A Glass Darkly	Frank Knaggs	99
Old Days Of Summer's Yield	M L Grabriele	100
The Adult Dinosaur	Patrick Humble	101
Think 'N' Act	Jean Horsham	102
Old Rover	Sylvia M Thompson	103
The Wind	Stephen Grant	104
My Children	Peter White	105

The Silver Swan	Angela Fishwick	106
Memories Of the Seaside	Cathy Thomas	107
Red	Jim Gardiner	108
Ian	J Lunn	109
Peace And Love	V Wood	110
Questions And Answers	G Richardson	11
Dark Secret	Joan Jemson	112
Betrayal	E Wilson	113
Daffodils	Lillian R Gelder	114
WFTB	Eleanor Pace	115
Men Without Their Boots	V Robson	116
Winter	Gemma Quinn	117
Into Tomorrow	Marie Ness	118
Meditation	Brenda Norman	119
Holidays	Sue Pine	120
Sisters	J S McKinney	121
The Magic Of Winter	D Cowan	122
Broken	Shawn W Le Gard	123
Every Toy Has Its Day	Eileen Potts	124
Arrival	T M Rutherford	125
My World Of Dreams	F P Collinson	126
Changing Times	Ruth Hughes	127
Vision Of The Blind	A Gormly	128
Childhood's End?	Martin Kenneth Watson	129
Insanity	Tania Marie Lowerson	130
The House	J B Wilkinson	131
Day Trip	James W Harvey	132
As A Cloud	Anne Chisholm	133
That Feeling!	Lynne Blakelock	134
Futuristic Thoughts	Alex Branthwaite	135
After The Gold Tarnished	Eric Karlson	136
Reminiscence	Doreen Baker	137
Far Away You	E Stephens	138
You	David E Colledge	139
For Your Eyes Only	John Cougle	140
Past The Longest Day	Duncan A Smith	141
I Am	Rebecca Minto	142

North East Memories	Mary Robinson	
Morning Shadows	R Tose	144
Life Is Cruel	H Bevan	145
A Poem Of Days In Many Ways	Robert John Temple	146
The Sea Is A Snake	Mark Wilkinson	147
The Fastest Slater In The West	Harry Ord	148

THE LAST REMAINING DREAM

There's a boy
Standing on a deserted beach
Throwing stones among the never-ending waves
And in another day's time
He won't remember
The good things they said about him
Only that he left
Leaving his friends on the inside
And he on the outside
Of his last remaining dream

The boy becomes a father
Forgets he used to be a child
Weighed down by the years
Where did all your beaches go
Who's throwing your stones now
Are the waves still coming

Funny how children make you forget
The parents you once had
Now you're on the inside
Watching a boy throwing stones on a beach
What was it like on the outside

Simon Downs

ON A LONELY MOOR

Grey stone ruins on a Northumbrian moor,
What tales of the past they could tell:
Would they talk of steel bonnet'd raiders
Or of brave men, in battle, who fell?

Would they tell you of times that they were hungry,
When their livestock was stolen in the night
And the sight of their burning houses,
Or their children crying out with fright?

Perhaps they would tell us of their happier times,
Although I think there would be few,
Or when peace reigned in this borderland
And there were no hoof-prints left in the dew:

Now, no jangling harness or clanking steel
No sword or dirk at hand,
No bands of raiding horsemen,
Now there is peace throughout this land.

And as I stand among these grey stone ruins
With their echoes from the past,
I felt for the moment, I knew these people
May they have their peace at last.

Brian Ducker

THE CONSTANT STAR

Long ago a sign was promised, to set free the hearts of men,
So a constant Star came shining, over little Bethlehem,
In a stable *oh so lowly*, came the Christ Child meek, and small,
Blessed shepherds were the first ones to proclaim Him Lord of all,
Constant Star forever shining, spread His message loud and clear,
Fill the hearts of men with wisdom, love and hope, not war and fear,
Start the joy bells loudly ringing, round the world both near and far,
So the people of all nations hear the message of that Star!
Unseen angels close around us, hope and pray with watchful mien.
Waiting, for the dawn of reason that will set the fires a-gleam,
In men's hearts, and start them longing for the all-consuming love,
Which is God's eternal promise of the constant Star above.

Robina Potter

THE MINER'S ETERNAL GLOW

He sits in his armchair by the side of the gas fire
No more the sound, of a crackling volcano
No flickering shadows fill the room
No spitting and splattering onto the carpet
No place to put the pokers, sticks or kettle
Only the glow as he sits silently,
Watching his favourite television show

He sits in his armchair by the side of the gas fire
His face no longer has a young man's glow
No dancing flames to sparkle and flash
His eyes a dull morbid, sadness show
Greying, yellow hair, thinning here and there
As he sits silently in the glow
Watching his favourite television show

He sits in his armchair by the side of the gas fire
Sometimes the tears they flow
When memories of a long time ago
Fan the embers of the past
To smoulder and ignite his soul
As he sits silently in the glow
Watching his favourite television show

He sits in his armchair by the side of the gas fire
Then he breathes his last breath,
Like the cinders from the fire,
Taken and laid to rest
Now another sits silently in the glow
Watching his favourite television

June Stainsby

CUT AND DASH?

Why *do* good hairdressers all disappear?
It's something that happens to me every year.
I get used to just one,
Turn around and they're gone
In a streak, (so to speak) it's so queer.

I go to a stylist for peace.
And that's why I liked sweet Denise.
So demure as she cut,
Shaped and blow-dried - oh! But
Our Denise, went to Greece (via Nice).

Jerome went to Rome, and John to Ceylon
And neither I wanted to lose.
Then Marie married Lee,
And they both went to sea
To couture all the rich, on a cruise.

So with Lisa in Pisa and Lorraine off to Spain
I'm lost for my highlights and dyes.
I refuse to have Chris,
(Such an impudent Miss)
And Jenny gets soap in my eyes.

What with Clarice in Paris and Joanne in Sudan
And Elaine took a plane to Bahrain.
What happened to Frieda
Just when I need her?
And Jane?
(On a train - Salisbury Plain!)

It'll have to be Vi. I'll give her a try.
As I sit with my hair soaking wet -
Did I hear Susan say
Vi walked out today
And took the last plane to Tibet?

Sylvia Gargett

BLUE FOR YOU

He cheers me up
when I am down
he makes me laugh
not sigh or frown
he's always there
whenever I'm blue
I call on him
he knows what to do
I know one day
he won't be here
and I'll be lost without my dear
although he knows
how much I care
it's not enough if only I dare
tell him how much he means to me
but it wouldn't be fair
because you see
he has three children
and a wife
and I don't want
to cause them strife
I know he feels
the way I do
and that is why
I'm feeling blue.

J Pounder

LEGACY OF THE TALL SHIPS

Dark evening mists of time and tide
swirling into the murky Tyne.
Came bringing ghosts of long ago
on wings of billowed canvas.

Perhaps they felt reborn these ships
as back into the womb they slipped.
But all was still in empty yards
and women toiled and waited.

We did not stint our welcoming
for pride still is a precious thing.
We could afford to celebrate
though empty pockets hung heavy.

Oak masts and spars with rigging taut
with plates and planks caulked as they aught.
Our men admired not grudgingly
their skills held in abeyance.

Unfurling sails and walking spars
cheers and salutes from modern tars.
Thrilling us with an age long gone
they left us by the river.

Could still the yards ring with the sound
of hammers that on steel do pound.
Shipbuilding men pass on your skills
the young ones now are learning.

Seafarers of the world at play
will bring work to the Tyne one day.
Boats for their pleasure we can build
we've always had the knowledge.

Ruth Henderson

CANNY SHIELDS

The town is known as Canny Shields
It's history stretches back,
And it is known throughout the world
To every seaman Jack.

Its past was lurid - purple - grim,
Exciting - boistering - rough,
Its people basic - hardworked - kind,
Warm-hearted - friendly - tough.

This was the town, a port indeed,
Where fishermen ploughed the deep
To gather harvest from the sea
For countless souls asleep.

There's not a trade it couldn't give
For shipbuilding on the Tyne,
And hundreds more were toiling
At a coalface, down a mine.

The town gave riggers and welders,
Platers - joiners - 'sparks',
Carpenters, riveters, plumbers,
Caulkers - painters - clerks.

Clive Street in its heyday
Had a cosmopolitan mix,
The world was represented
By the crews from countless ships.

This low street known world wide,
Was a stage for many parts,
Where life was played out, grim, and gay,
With tragedy and farce.

There's little left of Canny Shields
A new town grows up fast,
And now there's only memories
Of Canny Shields' colourful past.

Henry T Harris

A TIME OF WASTE

Discarding congealed curry in its foil fermenting tray,
Stripping off the shackles of a foul infernal day.
Retreat into your refuge, slump upon your old armchair,
Lethargy is your partner, no one knows or cares you're there.

Open text books at your feet nag at matters far more pressing,
Shrug the thought off; sod the lot, exams are just for guessing.
Dragging on a cigarette, slowly slide into a scene,
Where time stands still, and ancient silent ghosts enact a dream.

The world roams by regardless and oblivious of your pain,
Inside, you'd like to join it, but you can't be part again.
'Cos somehow you are annexed, though you look the same by day,
At night the image differs; mind reverses far away.

Smoke spirals wide to indicate cold comfort air invading,
The glow is warm and brighter still as outside light is fading.
Shake back the mind and draw the blind, dark walls come closing near,
Quickly switch onto the light; rush fast to fight the fear.

The spotlight almost blinds you; stare round as if all's treason,
Clear the chaos from your mind, and focus upon reason.
You slowly shake off dreamtime, put the cat out in the rain
Crawl into bed and wait until the circle starts again.

C M Nicholas

THE PRELUDE AND CONCLUSION TO LOVE

The commencement of the first encounter,
We were enchanted with each other.
The love began to blossom,
Together we enticed and seduced,
Your touch aroused every emotion,
Continually discovering one another.

But as the clock ticked in its incessant race of time,
The new-born love grew into a relationship,
An affinity between two people,
The enchantment remains,
Together their bond grew,
As did the bickering,
Each one progressively vulnerable,
The love advanced to pain.

The race began to slow and the clock continued ticking.
The bond began to dwindle,
And the enchantment disappeared,
They grasped and clutched to the fragments
And tore from the body that they'd shared,
Leaving a corpse with nothing to salvage,
Nothing left to be said,
They'd become two strangers,
Parallel to each other,
Looking back at it all,
Wondering exactly,
Where it was they went wrong.

Lisa McNee

SAILERS WEAR WHITE RIBBONS

I was standing in a doorway,
as she came strolling by.
I gave a little whistle,
to try and catch her eye.
She turned and smiled politely
and shook her golden hair.
Although my ship was leaving,
I know true love was there.
Love letters passed between us,
our words, so fond and true,
kissed each other daily,
across the oceans blue.
I asked her in a letter
if she would marry me
and on returning safely home
I went down on one knee.
We got a special licence,
next day we were a pair.
White ribbons on my uniform
white ribbons in her hair.
Those ribbons tied us sixty years
until she had to leave,
I'll miss her till I close my eyes
and then I'll cease to grieve.
For somewhere she is waiting
and again we'll be a pair,
white ribbons on my uniform
white ribbons in her hair.

Creative Writing Group
Adult Resource Service
North Tyneside

WORLD

You lead me into heavens
Unexplored by man.
The desert in my soul
Becomes the Promised Land.
You're the shimmer of a sunrise,
The moonlight on a pier.
Why should I ever want to go?
I've got the world right here.

Karen Manning

JOHN DOE

Lay me to rest, bid me rest in peace . . .
I sense your doubt
You question my worth
What fiend was I that I slipped away unmissed, unclaimed
(Was there ever a man so completely unloved?)
I feel your shame
Who are you to judge?
My anonymity is my eternal defence
(But I would have you know my soul was ruined)
Society asked,
Urged . . . petitioned . . . *demanded* . . .
Yet I could give nothing, for I had nothing to give
(No talent, no joy, no virtue)
Guilt
Effused over my brow, christened me worthless
I could not justify myself!
(So I was shown the evanescence of my mortality)
The exchange was made
My contemptible life, my ravaged body, my damned soul
For hazy, indolent peace.

Elaine Jobson

YOU ARE NOW

You are now . . .
        The whisper of an image
        A flutter of memory's wing.
        A gentle fleeting moment,
        A song to silently sing.

You are now . . .
        A misted breath of history
        A special 'sometimes' thought
        An elusive floating vision
        That never can be caught.

You are now . . .
        A dream that only surfaces
        In silence and solitude
        When with sadness and happiness
        You and I once more are fused

You are now . . .
        A swift and special instant
        A scent, a sound, a sigh
        It's all that's left to remind me
        Of the love we could only deny.

Liz Dinsdale

A MOTHER'S ASPIRATIONS

Son you are so beautiful,
A sight to behold,
I look at you in wonder,
What the future will hold.

A mother can see,
What other people cannot see,
Expectations not reality.
This child could become almost anything one day,
A famous writer,
A movie star,
Or even the President,
These things could happen,
These things could be,
A mother's imagination is extraordinary.

A mother looks at her child,
And at that moment,
And at that time,
The future looks just fine.

Happiness is what I want for him,
Of course a little money,
Intellectual ability,
A chance of suitability,
To fit into where he will want to be,
The future seems fine to me.

S L Johnston

CAPTIVE THOUGHTS

His thoughts and my thoughts merge,
I have freedom, he is captive.
Black as night, gleaming form, golden-eyed,
Not yet dead, not yet subdued.
Pacing his torment for all to see.
I watch, oh how I watch,
Afraid of his power, at one with his mind.
He approaches, glowing ebony frame,
Panting, scowling and finds my eyes.
Clear and mirrored the image of myself,
Held transfixed in gold.
Deep into the liquid pool,
On and on to distant lands,
Forbidden past, foreboding future.
On and on into a drifting mystic void.
I see the beast, it senses me!
Not knowing whether he returns the sight,
Whether he even cares,
Or acknowledges my existence.
I am as the mists of time
In eyes of disdaining response,
Through me and beyond.
I cannot avert my eyes and dare not blink;
He will not avert his.
My worth in doubt, I am extinct.
Bonding in passion and sympathy,
Bonded by rage
Me in my freedom
He in his cage!

Ian Richardson

SEA FOLK

My mother said when I was young come sit upon my knee
I'll tell you tales of other folk who dwell beneath the sea
They live in shells all pearly-white and dine on seaweed stew
Their cooking pots are limpets they must rinse them through and through
Seahorses take them off to school they have to learn their scales
For later on they sing in choirs with porpoises and whales
Mermaids and Mermen come to call they often stay for tea
They loll about and talk about their neighbours in the sea

. . . My dears, those noisy lobsters with their bagpipes and their flutes!
And what about those turtles with their tuning forks and lutes?
And have you seen those urchins who hang about and shout?
And tease the little sticklebacks when school is coming out . . . !

But all too soon it's time to go they have to get their sleep
They sway in little hammocks to the rhythm of the deep
They dream of treasures, trinkets and the songs their mothers taught
And what their world is coming to and who will come to naught

My mother said now have you liked the tales that I have told
Of other folk beneath the sea who dress in green and gold
And if you want to see them then you must bide near the shore
They come sometimes to see their kin who live here by the score
And if you meet them bow your head and ask them how they do
For the other folk are friendly folk and will stay forever true

Josie Brink-Jones

THE OTHER SIDE OF WAR

The other side of war
Shows blood - spilled-out guts - the gore,
When rocket shells blast from nowhere
Arms and legs fly into the air
The head and body not to be found
Only blood and guts cover the ground.

For King/Queen and Country; forces galvanised
Shown as victors over the despised.
TV films capture them on tape
But not victorious armies causing rape.

When the aftermath is swept
The other side of war is death.

For only the lucky few are left.
The rest vanquished in the soil beneath.

Albert Shepherd

THE MINER

I live, unlike my brother men
As I search around for coal
Artificial light is all I have
In this dark, dank earthy hole
For I'm a miner, and like a worm
I burrow in the earth
My father, and grandad before
Knew this right from my birth
A mining family, living there
In 'Geordie land', by Tyne
The right to hew coal from the seams
Was always meant as mine
It's better far since my dad's day
Machines help men like me
For as he crouched and worked away
There was barely glow to see
Hacking there, with blackened face
His pick in tired, torn hands
While up above, in skies so blue
We kids played on the sands
In these years, I've grown with coal
My body oft tired and worn
But I'm a miner, heart and soul
Since the day that I was born
And what I know above all else
With coal dust instead of tan
As I work my way - my dad will say
'You're a miner -you're a *man*.'

Epilogue:
And I'll say to dad, 'Now what's in store?
What will we do when the pit's *no more*?'

W Harmon

GOD'S HEROES

The year was nineteen forty,
On board a merchant ship.
The boy was fourteen years of age,
And it was his first trip.

The ship would be torpedoed,
And the boy would lose his life.
One in four of all such men,
Would not survive the strife.

For in the merchant service,
Men got little praise,
They had not smart uniforms,
For compliments to raise.

The ships had little armourment,
To chase the vicious foe.
Wages were pathetic,
These men had little dough.

The girls went for the other men,
With medals on their chests,
M N men in civvy suits,
Did not attract the rest.

Most of post-war services,
Where veterans parade,
Had little room for men like these,
Which makes them a charade.

But when the heavenly roll call comes,
When God calls out the praise,
That young merchant navy lad,
Will share His loving gaze.

Sean O'Halon

WHY?

Three more died, then three more.
The mourners wait outside the door.
Inside the house is grief and sorrow.
Will more people die tomorrow?

The war goes on and on, it seems.
Reporters write it up in reams.
People meet and make a pact.
More people will die, that's a fact.

Top men meet to talk, about talks, again!
Yet still the bomb blasts kill and maim.
Innocent children, young and and old
Die of hunger and the cold.

Other countries send their aid.
With this they think their debt is paid.
They were paid more to provide
The means by which more people died.

When greed for power reigns supreme
Opposing sides forget the dream
That one day all the wars will cease.
The whole wide world will live in peace.

John Robert Ingram

REMEMBRANCE

His love has gone, no more I'll see
His worn and wrinkled face,
In times of trouble, he was with me,
But now has left this, race.
He's out in a rainbow, high in the sky,
His tired spirit, free,
I never thought one day he would die,
And not be with me.
But now he's gone, and I have, no dad,
No old one to love,
He's far away, my old man,
But in spirit, he's just a lad.

Rachel Oxtoby

OUR BLUE-EYED LUCKY

I am a tabby and quite cuddly,
And bonny, beautiful and lovely.
Little Lucky lost her Mum
Because her owner didn't want her as a chum.
Into the field she was thrown,
Looking sad and all forlorn,
Luckily she was found, safe and sound and only three weeks old.
Now she is queen who wears a crown.
'Lucky' is my name, and I'm a lucky girl I came,
I've found two mums, who spoil me, and give me every attention.
And in return she gives so much love and affection.
She's a beautiful white-chested tabby, tinted with gold,
Found a new home and no longer out in the cold.
She lives like one of the best, and plays football like Georgie Best.
I've a beauty spot at the end of my nose,
And a big heart which goes down to my toes.

E Pickthall

VISIONS

Looking through a camera what do I see?
The sun casting shadows on the old oak tree
Or a field full of rich yellow rape
My eyes take in the beauty of our landscape.

On four wheels I travel many miles a day
Taking pictures whatever comes my way
From a wild bunch of flowers
To a rainbow of colours, in between showers.

Walking I see things in a different light
Sparkling dew on a spider's web
To a glowing moon at night
An aerial view of a river winding far below
Or maybe a range of hills covered in snow.

Pictures of rooftops, chimney-stacks all different sizes
Watching the grey smoke pollute the air as it rises
Then my eye catches the freshness of a waterfall
Or the breeze as it catches the reeds already tall

The innocent face of a child to the reality of an old man's
The mark of hard times, the truth lies in his hands
People smiling, laughing or with tears in their eyes
Every picture tells a story - a camera never lies.

Jean Cumbor

A RESIDENCE

Mam
and Dad
And I made three.
In my own bedsit I'd be.
The man
Of my dreams,
Had impossible schemes
Me and my spouse built a house,
Along
Came Timmy
And little Kay,
A garden they needed
In which they could happily play,
So now
We are moving
Once again - to a villa in Spain.
My children have grown - from the nest they have flown.
Now
I'm
Retired. My husband expired.
Our cottage in the country never transpired.
No more will I roam,
My residence
Is now a 'home'.

Mary Wright

ON THE WALK TO CAUSEY ARCH BEAUTY SPOT

She must have hated herself, to risk
awful injuries, worse than death,
plunging like a bag of garden-waste.
Or was it a sense of justice she had
to take the consequences?

Did she just practice, edge too far?
Was she drunk, full of pills, or both? Certainly
'downers' would make the plan more comfortable;
and 'uppers'? Euphoric mood; to float perhaps?
To fly to where dreams are made?

Nobody pushed her, not by physical means.
No question of it; Coroner's report said so:
Balance of mind disturbed. Notes are convenient,
tucked beneath stones: spider-scrawled over
old Asda bills for milk, beans, bread.

The family was asked. It was circumstances:
pain of living greater than act of dying.
Extinction. Out of it. Out from this cinder-path
launch, crunching years underfoot, breathing
last of rhododendrons, sweet as promises.

The geographic whereabouts are well-known
to enthusiasts, snapping photographic detail
hoping the light is right, trusting
the angle. Wary, they marvel
at the drop.

Heather L Young

PEACE IN THE END

Our dreams of peace for this precious land,
Are slapped in the face by man's cruel hand,
The plans we made . . . no longer valid,
Buildings ruined, cities squalid,
Bombs and bullets exploding salvoes,
Blasting death and pain to the hearts of our heroes.

As men of honour fall to the ground,
War wreaks its havoc all around,
Soldiers dying in their prime,
Never to know peace in their time.

Loyal and true they'll die for their cause,
As forward they march thro' death's open doors,
Taking only the best as it constantly proves,
That death is the victor, whilst the rest of us lose.

We've come full circle in man's evolution,
Could this really be the final solution?
Will mankind fall and stumble t'wards its own execution?
And is this the Act of divine retribution?

For all the years we've made war in His name,
To cleanse the earth of this evil strain?
Destroyed and beaten by God's mighty hand,
We didn't deserve this beautiful land,
Now the fighting will cease . . . Behold! Only peace,
For it's what we all wanted, a final release . . .

Epilogue:
Now the world is as it was before,
No pain nor hurt nor talk of war,
We thank the Lord for our daily bread,
And the peace that abounds . . .
Now that we are all dead!

Esther Wilson

TOBRUK 1941
(Written in Tobruk, Christmas 1941)

Now that the dawn is near,
Please God, help me overcome my fear,
All night the flash of gunfire has lit the sky,
All night in battle order, ready we lie
Come the dawn, we shall meet the attacking foe,
And all hell, both foe and defender will know.

My thoughts this night, are not of this desert sand,
But of Durham, my home county, in England,
How green its fields, how proud its peoples,
How deep the denes, how tall its steeples;
My memory flows along with every turn of the River Wear,
Every colliery village, town, and the city, I see so clear.

The day is dawning, and light is here,
I'm afraid of death, and sick with fear,
The squeak of tank tracks, that yet I cannot see,
And I know, they are followed by enemy infantry,
Many this day the full price will pay,
Must I too, die in this wasteful way?

We held our fire, until aim was true,
Then came the command, fire, to every gun crew,
The enemy took heavy casualties as they entered a gap,
Successfully caught in cross-fire, by well-prepared trap,
All day long the conflict swayed to and fro,
Then we fixed bayonets, ammunition was low.

The battle is over, the enemy in retreat,
A young German soldier lies dead at my feet,
For life or death, we had fought hand to hand,
For nothing more than a hole in the sand,
He lies so still, staring, yet cannot see,
I had to kill you, or you would have killed me.

I never thought that a soldier I would be,
Defending Tobruk, with my back to the sea,
We live like rats, in every cranny and nook,
And Rommel has called us the Rats of Tobruk,
This name we will keep, and hold with pride,
For we have held Tobruk, and halted Rommel in his stride.

G T Vincent

FOR A MOMENT

Let me, for a moment,
Feel the sunshine, see the sky.
I'm young, just born and from my birth
I've been condemned to die.

Let me, for a moment,
Graze on pasture, feel the rain,
Just give me time to live a while
And I'll not ask again.

Let me, for a moment
Feel my mother's gentle breath
And nuzzle up against her
Before I face my death.

Let me, for a moment
Do what youngsters do.
Play, be free with all my friends
That's all I ask of you.

Let me, for a moment
Banish all my fear,
It's cramped, it's dark, I can't move much
I'm frightened locked in here.

Please do not, for a moment,
Forget what lies ahead
The crate, the men, the journey
Then I'll soon be dead.

Will you, for a moment
Spare a thought for me,
And what my future holds
If things are left to be.

Will you, for a moment
Act on my behalf
And question those who legislate
The future of the calf.

Jackie Pass

DOWN THE PIT

So down you trudge again
As you begin your shift
With your mucky clothes and headlamp
As you head towards the lift

Another long night awaits you
Deep down beneath the ground
With your little canary in his cage
With his nervous chirpy sound

You keep your eyes upon him
You both are scared of gas
But there's nothing there, you can smell
Just a dark and filthy mass

You soon pick out the rockface
Where you spend the night in toil
As you scrape the skin off your hands
In the heat your sweat does boil

The whistle blows, you give a sigh
Praying you'll see the morning sky
With aching limbs you collect your friend
Another shift is at its end.

K Riley

THE ALARM CLOCK

From the moment I was born the clock was set for me
And the hands of time started moving irrevocably.
The pendulum swung to and fro to the sound of a loud tick tock
And my span in life was measured by the hands on the face of the clock.
Time seemed unimportant when I was still a child
But youth brought impatience, time's slowness drove me wild.
It often seemed to me that the clock had changed its speed
In reality it ticked steadily on through whatever fate decreed.
If only the clock would stop awhile so that happiness would last
But it was then it seemed to gather speed and moved on much too fast.
Yet the hours dragged by endlessly on days of strife and sorrow
The cogs turned the wheels meticulously into another sad tomorrow.
The pendulum still swung back and forth with each monotonous beat
Propelling me ever forward with no chance of retreat.
Time suddenly took wing as older in years I grew
And I realised my remaining years numbered but a few.
Soon I knew the alarm would ring of that there was no doubt
Then the clock would run down and stop, finally worn out.

Marjorie Edgar

PRIDE 1995

One day; just one day
for us.
A day to celebrate rejection
as we call for acceptance.

We sing, we dance, we play,
we laugh.

We share, we pray, we mourn,
we cry.

A day of opposites,
of paradoxes.

A day perfectly me.

Damien Whiter

THE STARS AT NIGHT

Those stars at night how they twinkle and shine
A sight to behold as I walk by the Tyne
Just like sparkling diamonds on a black velvet cape
Their perpetual beauty depicts the enigma of space.

Ann Watson

NOTHING CHANGES

The young boy in his patched short trousers
And the prematurely old man in his cloth cap
Walk along the riverside, hand in hand,
And the child's eyes widen
At the sight of the unfinished boat lying like a beached whale,
Surrounded by the sound of silence and the smell of the Tyne,
Whilst he inwardly ponders the answer his granda gave him
When he asked why nobody was working today.
But try as he might, he can't understand why the man
Said 'money' so bitterly,
And spat on the ground with such disgust.

Granda, why don't you go to work now?
The man with the coal dust lined face
Stares down at the child in his mended shorts, for a while
Remembering how he once asked his granda a similar question,
And he unconsciously re-enacts the scene
As he replies 'money' with bitterness in his voice,
Before spitting to one side in disgust,
While the child looks on in puzzlement.

The young boy in his smart jeans and expensive trainers
Tugs impatiently at his granda's hand,
Wishing he was home in the warmth, with his computer,
Instead of having to listen to this old man
Rambling on about the pits and shipyards.
And as he begins to curse man's old god 'money',
The child sighs,
And turns towards the horizon,
Against which the metal dinosaurs and the pit heap
Stand darkly silent in the fast fading twilight,
Savouring the smell and sound of silence.

C A Lewis

BEFORE THE SPARTANS CAME TO BLYTH

Before the Spartans came to Blyth, or magpies were full grow'd,
A little Geordie drunkard made the famous Scotswood road.
A rambing road, a shambling road, that wanders up and down
And after him the polis ran, the bailiff, half the town.
A merry road, a boozy road, where we did drink your fill
The night we we walked to Gallowgate by way of Rowlands Gill.

I've had no truck with bailiffs, I've never struck a copper,
And if I took on half the town I'd come a right old cropper.
But I would bash their heids in if they should come array'd
To straighten out the crooked road that drunken Geordie made.
Where you would see wor lad and me with broon ale in our hands
The night we went to James's Park by way of Tynemouth Sands.

His sins they were forgiven him, or why do boozers thrive
To gan alang the Scotswood Road like when he was alive?
He staggered forth from left to right and knew not which was which
But the Blue Star shone above him when they found him in the ditch.
So pardon us, nor harden us, we did not see so clear
The night we went to Roker Park by way of South Shields pier.

My friend, we may not go again to see the Blaydon races
And watch the lads and lasses there with bright and smiling faces.
But I will walk beside you to St James's Leazes End
And shout aloud 'Howay the lads - Newcassels's won agen!'
For there are cup ties to be played, and finals to be seen
Before we go to paradise by way of Jesmond Dene.

E Barnett

MY SECRET PLACE

Secret place
Open wide, and inside
A meadow gay
With birds at play,
All is green
And I've seen
The Fairy Queen,
Through one tunnel
Without a funnel
Past a range,
Then into a fairy
I will change.

Sylvia Sinclair

IGNORANCE 2000

Nearly 2000 years on and what have we learned
'Not a thing,' we still hate we still kill,
We refuse to love, refuse to believe, we do what we will
As man and woman we were designed to love one another.
But we still lie and cheat, and betray each other.
'2000 years and what have we learned?'
We haven't yet!
We still go to war we destroy what we can
And what's it all for!
We lie and fight with one another and our children rebel
We will have to learn soon, or we may as well all be in hell.
2000 years ago we murdered God's Son!
Now He shows us what we achieved exactly what we won!
What did we gain on that day but sorrow.
Poverty, hardship, bad health, death and we
All pray for a new tomorrow.
2000 years and what have we learned, nothing
But to destruct our minds and hearts, and slowly expel mankind.
We were given commandments to follow ten basic
Rules delivered and signed.
Man and woman broke every one of them by disbelief.
Even our sexes are at war, and our countries
Still battle to conquer, to cause pain and grief.
2000 years on and what have we learned,
Our world is dying! Our ignorance with
Chemicals and nuclear bombs show
What we have done from east to west!
We listen, but to our political leaders,
Who says they know best?
Now we must know, now we must listen
And learn from God! We must open our eyes and see!
2000 years now! We must accept, we must believe
It's simple, Bible principle and love for God
Is the only key!

G Burton

A PRAYER FOR GLENN

You were taken from me
While so very young,
You were such a lovely baby,
My one and only son.
I didn't hold you in my
Arms for very long,
And now you're with the angels
Listening to their nursery song.
Your sisters all send you their love,
And I know you are smiling at
Us from above.
I keep wondering each day
If the pain will go away,
But deep in my heart I
Know it's here to stay.
I know that I can never bring you back
And I must walk down this long
And lonely track.
I see my daughters grow up,
And see all the things they do,
And I know that in each of them there
Is a part of you.

Carol Renneberg

SNAPSHOT MEMORIES OF MY MOTHER

Searching through a dusty drawer
I find her ring, and palming it,
feel again the cutting edge of grief,
as snapshot memories reel through my mind
of times long dead.

Snap

Sucking my thumb, I sit on her knee
as she reads aloud the Tales of Rupert Bear
from yellow hard backed Mary Tourtell books.

Snap

Playing in a war time street I hear her shout
'Am going to the pictures. Want to come?'

A hundred films we queued to see,
my Mum and I.

Snap

I'm running home from school,
along the lane and down the hill
to where she is always waiting, tea ready.
Together we listen to Children's Hour.
Our favourites - Worzel Gummidge, Toytown.

Snap

On winter evenings we sit side by side,
knitting coloured squares
for a blanket for my doll.

Snap

The memories are positive,
so I reel them in,
before the negatives begin.

Doreen Dean

BIRDS OF A FEATHER

Both long-tailed black and white,
They visit frequently.
Gliding in swift of wing,
I watch them constantly.

Perched resting for a while,
At last they end their flight.
Bright eyed hopping down the path,
Much to my delight.

Now whose arriving not Mr Crow,
He's always over-zealous.
Spying them obviously a couple,
He'll be a little jealous.

He's trying to get close,
We all know three's a crowd.
Finding himself being ignored,
He exits very proud.

Away he soars from on high
He views them like he's royal.
Plain to see it's two for joy,
This pair are free but loyal.

Elsie Scrowther

A FATHER

My father was a patriot, or so I am told,
Summoned from his children's games . . .

    . . . One lazy Sunday after tea.

To serve the needs of unknown men,
To a distant place too far removed,
From lingering kiss on childhood cheek,
And unfinished battles on the living room floor.

For he was gentle, he was kind,
A warm blanket in which to hide,
No soldierly figure did he portray,
As he slowly walked away . . .

    . . . One lonely Sunday after tea.

Newspaper reports of victories won,
Of warrior bravery and courageous deed,
No media space for childlike fears,
Fatherhood forgotten at warlike speed.

Objectives achieved, triumphant return,
Every man a hero in the eyes of the crowd,
For tear stained eyes through frosted glass,
No fathers return down garden path . . .

    . . . One cold Sunday after tea.

My father was a patriot, or so I am told,
He was my father and nothing more.

K S Pringle

THEY KNEW NOT WHY

None but the brave carried on,
Others deserted, they were gone.
The war was young, yet men grew old,
From unending pressures of combat and stress.
The world no more they could understand,
Their lives meant nothing now,
But once, they knew it was grand.
Called up were they to fight for their land,
Each man and boy were asked to make a stand.
They fought for country, King and Queen,
Yet, knew not why they fought.
Each soldier equipped with weapon to kill,
But soon with war, each had their fill.
Sickened inside by sight of death,
The weak fled, while those who stayed,
Young and old alike, were slayed.
War had dealt a crippling blow,
But for attacked, aggressor, brave and deserter,
Mercy unto them the Lord will show.
For they knew not why they fought.

Kenneth Storey

JUST AN OLD HEAP

There you stand draped in your cloak
so green, an old pit heap, blot on the
landscape.
That is how the locals see you,
I see you so differently though,
I see you as the children climb
to your top, I hear them scream
with delight as they roll to your
bottom, you see you are their Everest.
A fall of snow and you are transformed
a ski slope, the children dressed in
bright colours dragging reluctant parents
pulling sledges, carrying old tin trays,
a Turner painting brought to life.

Now it is spring, my turn to climb to your
top. I sit with my little dog, closing my eyes.
I let the stresses and strains of life float
away.
A breeze plays with my hair, an orchestra
of sound reaches my ears, magpies chatter,
a crow adds his voice, the train blows its
hooter as it races towards the station.
Sheep call anxiously to their lambs, I open
my eyes fully to see a rabbit on his hind legs.
Who is more surprised, him or me! He hops off
to his burrow, white tail bobbing.
I look to the power station belching smoke,
teased by the breeze like cotton wool floating in the sky,
trees and fields yellow and green.
The church steeple rises above Cramlington
village, the steeple once used as a lookout for
marauders from the sea. No, this pit heap is
special, special to me.

Sylvia Rook

THE CHILD WHO IS BORN TODAY

He comes into the great big world
And is placed on his mother's breast.
She smiles at him and holds him tight
The joy she cannot suppress.

He looks around and wonders why
'Why am I here?'
Then a soundless cry comes from his lips
Of unknowingness and fear.

The next few minutes are timeless
As he's passed around the room.
The child he starts to wish that he
Was back in his mother's womb.

There it was peaceful, and safe too,
The darkness was all around.
But the child he felt so secure
Hearing his mother's gentle sounds.

And yet here he is to start with us
His life from a baby all the way,
Until he becomes an adult
He is the child who was born today.

Sarah Atkin

THE BEST THINGS IN LIFE ARE FREE

They say the best things in life are free
For some of us this is not the case
The best things only come after
A lot of heartache and sacrifice.

Norman Guthrie

PALLION CAN WORK

Sunderland was once a shipbuilding town,
The yards the Tories have long since closed down,
No ships now are launched at the Pallion Quay
To sail down the river and into the sea.

The Northeast has the best workforce we know,
So let them to the shipyards go.
Come on Tories give the yards the test,
We know they can produce the best.

Just like Swans 'Pallion can work',
So come on Tories give yourself a jerk,
Let Pallion do the job they know the best.
'Pallion can work' and pass the shipbuilding test.

So let Sunderland be a shipbuilding city,
The ships they build will be oh so pretty
And let them be launched at the Pallion Quay
And sail down the river and into the sea.

David Reynoldson

FIRE

The sound of crackling wood, and a soft wave
of smoke that drifts out of the window.
I stood there entranced, as the mixture of
red and orange flames rose higher and higher.
By then it was too late to do anything!
Smoke billowed out of every window, the heat
was incredible!
Flames that seemed to have come out of
nowhere, were leaping from the ground floor to the first.
Suddenly, the whole house was ablaze.
The next moment, three fire engines come
hurtling around the corner, sirens screaming.
In a matter of minutes the fire was out,
the fire engines had gone and an eerie silence
filled the street.
I stood there and watched the remains of my home.
A pile of rubble.

Katie O'Brien (12)

THE CARDBOARD HOTEL

Some years ago, I remember quite well,
A few down, and out's, at the 'Cardboard Hotel'
Sleeping out rough in the wind and the rain,
Not knowing if they'll ever, see daylight again,
Some sitting round fires, to keep themselves warm,
Others, burning their beds and doing no harm,
Drinking, whiskey! Meths! Or rum! And brown ale!
Amongst cardboard coffins, and liquid nails.
They're on their way out, if they only knew,
But they're only human, just like me and you!
The 'Cardboard Hotel' was the old council yard,
For those poor down and out's, their existence was hard!

Stephen Wainwright Brown

THE POEM I COULDN'T WRITE

The teacher said 'I have a treat
As we've had such a hard working day.
I want you all to write a poem
So we can finish in a very nice way.'

Great, I thought, yes, wopee,
Mine will be the best in the class!
I'd go as far to even say
If this were an exam, I'd pass.

The poem, now what could it be about?
Oh help, I haven't a clue!
I'm going to get totally murdered,
If I don't have a thing to do.

I've now been sat here 20 minutes,
And I haven't even got a name,
Help, the teacher's coming over,
It'll be like shoot 'em game.

Phew, she didn't see what I've done yet,
But 10 minutes and then I'll be dead!
I've got to think of something quick.
If only I had a different brain in my head.

The seconds are ticking down now,
Hang on - no need to fear,
Quite suddenly, out of the blue
I've had an amazing idea.

Why don't I write what happened today,
It's funnier than the way I bat,
And yes, if you haven't already guessed,
What you've just read is that!

Laura Graham

TO MY GIRLFRIEND

As far away as the farthest star,
as close as your silken hair,
at the dawn of each day
at the close of each night,
you will find my love there.

It will never be known,
excepting by you
and I doubt that the world really cares,
but as long as you know,
if you hold out your hand,
my love will always be there.

I love you.

Michael Griffith

MEMORIES

'What did you do in the war, Gran? What did you do in the war?'
Well, my heart gave a lurch, and I stared into space.
And I thought of the shock to the whole human race,
Of the pain and the sorrow the destruction and despair,
How we cowered in shelters as bombs screamed through the air.

Then I thought of the good times, of good neighbours and friends,
Of the songs that we sang waiting for air-raids to end
And the hundreds of letters to a man far away
Of the queues for bananas, it could be your lucky day
And I thought of the closeness of the caring of folk, all wanting to help,
                                              all willing to talk.

And I thought of Lord Woolton and American dried eggs
And the gravy browning to paint on our legs
And we did have laughter and we did have fun
We sang silly songs like 'Run, Rabbit, Run'
And we listened to 'ITMA' and all did our bit
And the Radio Doctor kept us all fit.

We cheered Monty and the soldiers he led
And we longed for one quiet night to sleep in our beds
And we listened to Churchill's rallying speeches when he urged us to fight
                                              on the land and the beaches
I remember Dame Vera with love and affection
And Glen Miller's band and the lovely Anne Shelton.

So never forget all those brave fighting boys
The memories bring pain but also some joys.
And when we have a bit grouse as we're all wont to do
Let us think of the sacrifice that brought us all through
So celebrate after 50 long years
We must sing and be glad, it's no time for tears.

Agnes Summerbell

ODE TO A DEAD LOVE

Cold, cold the grave, where dead love lies,
Gone are the whispers, and the sighs,
Gone the gentle hands, and the kiss
Gone the sweet caress, and the bliss
                           of giving,
All is dead that once was living.

Still, still the heart, that once would beat
With exultation when we'd meet,
The silence hovers o'er me now,
My head bends low, and so I bow
                           to sorrow,
Knowing there is no tomorrow.

Cruel, cruel to leave me thus alone,
To know not how I can atone,
No use to weep, you would not hear,
Nor yet pay heed or shed a tear
                           of woe,
For one who could not let you go.

Bleak, bleak, the days that lie ahead,
All has been done, all is now said,
I cannot share, I must not blame,
No more pleading, gone is the shame,
                           for see,
I let you go, I set you free.

Zoe Grant

THE ESCAPE

The day has come for my great escape.
My life is coming to its start.
The comfort of these warm waters, will soon be gone.
My hermit existence, no more

The journey now begins, pushing me down.
I'm leaving this safe cocoon forever.
The thrill of this adventure, I can hardly contain.
I'm nearly there, I feel the tension.

I hope that I will be what they want.
The light is blinding me, I begin to blink.
I let out a small cry, just to show I'm here.
The world seems a bit chaotic at present.

A warm and delicious smell is in my nostrils.
A loving voice speaks in whispers.
A smile seen through a veil, greets me.
Hello Mum, I'm pleased to meet you.

Gillian Heron

PEACE

Peace, it seems, has been restored,
gone are the words that sting,
we sit back and smile, like two tigers.
Ready to spring.

Jude Ratcliffe

NORTH LANDING

I cast my eyes down the well worn path
Showing patches of brown through the green.
It twists, and turns on its lofty way
On cliffs skirting the seascape scene.

The heritage trail rises and dips
Like the seagulls on the wing,
And in places almost overlooks
Where the sea, its treasures bring.

I pause awhile, and scan the view
Looking across the bay.
Yachts with sails a-flapping
Cruising on their way.

The morning sun in its brilliance
Gave an iridescent glow
To the surface of the ocean
Where the seabirds were diving low.

A sudden swoop by a gull in flight
As it sees a silvery streak
Causing rippling whirls in the water
Then thrusting skywards, its catch in its beak.

I watched as the gull headed shorewards
The fish struggling with a silent raving.
Climbing, then banking, and dropping
To its nest on the cliff-face haven.

I could only imagine the welcome
As the chicks with their mouths so wide,
Squawking, impatiently waiting,
Till the gull thrusts each piece inside.

This scenario is endlessly repeated
Time after time in their quest.
From the first finger of light at daybreak,
Till the sinking of the sun in the west.

Ron Marriott

INDIAN SUMMER

Near Dunstanburgh, there is a bay
A very little bay,
Where you and I sat quietly
One fine October day.

That little bay had silver sand,
And sky and sea were blue,
The sea's edge rimmed with silver waves
And shells were silver too.

And high above were silver wings
Of seabirds in full flight,
And earth and sea were bathed that day
In autumn's golden light.

Margery Baston

SEARCHING FOR NABOKOV

Turning pages,
I trace the lines
from your pen,
tapping out the trip
your tongue makes
down the palate,
to tap, at three,
on the teeth -
Lo. Lee. Ta.

Amidst mimosa,
I strain to hear
the sea carrying
whispered words;
stolen kisses, coupled
with biscuity embraces,
combine in the murmur -
Lo. Lee. Ta.

Somewhere, he must end
and leave only you,
delighting in the taste of
chocolate glacé, lingering
still on seaside lips.
And later, is it you
lying in surrender;
trembling under soft strokes,
devouring little girl limbs,
 amidst the echo of
Lo. Lee. Ta?

Tanya Winter

THOUGHTS OF A REDUNDANT SIGNALMAN

Rust red among the weeds, metals that
Once mirrored the sky,
Pane-shattered windows of decaying signal box nearby,
No sounds of hissing steam and whistling for attention,
No more smells of burning oil and blackened smoke from engine,
Gone is the station once heart of the town,
The platforms are dust, the bridges are down.

Death to the railway and long live the road,
No need to protest at the increasing load
Of cars and lorries with poisoned emissions
And growing list of dead from bad collisions,
The wise Doctor Beeching's pill was swallowed whole,
Branch lines to close, railmen on the dole,
Station staff and signalmen conversant with the rules
Platelayers, gangers and their men lay down their tools.

Today, retired, I walk the paths where once were stations
And trains controlled by signals, rules and regulations,
I see the piles of household rubbish uncollected
And wonder why life's progress makes me so dejected.

J Alcock

TREASURE

Jamie is my grandson
Worth more to me than gold.
He makes me very happy
And stops me feeling old.

Jamie is my diamond
His eyes shine like the stars
In his world of make believe
Playing with his cars

Jamie is my pearl
Of that there is no doubt.
When his arms go round my neck
I know what love is all about.

Jamie is my treasure,
The best jewel by far.
I am so very lucky
That I am his grandma.

G Williams

DILEMMA

In these hands that are cupped together
        lies a butterfly
The question is, should I let it go?
For if I keep it
        it will surely die
Yet because I would be left with its beauty
Would the fact that it's dead
Truly
        sadden my heart

Silken wings beat frantically against
        the palms of my hands
A life so short, a mate to find
The question becomes
        what will my conscience stand?
Could I live with just the memory of its beauty
Would the joy of parting
Truly
        gladden my heart

John Mears

HOW DOES SHE FEEL

How does she feel lonely
for she lives not alone,
she has a husband and
her children's noisy drone,

How can she be bored
she has plenty to do,
dishes to the ceiling
washing on the floor too,

How can she feel tired
that's what a woman's for,
going out to work
coming home to the chores,

Why does she need
someone to talk to
the telly's on full,
it can't answer back
is that so dull,

Why does she talk to
herself, is she going mad,
she's getting an answer
is that so bad.

Trudy Appleby

KEEP SMILIN' THROUGH

After blitz of Heinkels
Raking
Quickened leaves from thunder,
Flowered flame lit primrose
On a thousand battered homes.
Anathema found morning
As the town was torn asunder -
And scattered ash spread everywhere,
But monuments and domes
Were saved.
Then out of the railway catacombs
. . . From London's shelters,
Life returned
Through mounting rubble,
Shards of glass,
Where fallen ranks of streets were burned
By bombs and booming
Gas;
But bird song echoed from the trees
Recalling
Sweeter times than these.

. . . And while tin-hatted rescue men
Raised ladders to the sky,
A quiet king (in wellingtons)
Showed war the reason why.

Bernard M Jackson

THE POET AND THE LECTURER

There's a university lecturer who
tomorrow I will meet
I hope the hell we're on the same
planet
cos we ain't in the same street.

And oh boy am I scared?
Yes, that scared I just go numb
I'm not illiterate or thick, but,
compared with this guy I'm plain
dumb.

He, has letters after his name
even if they're not hung on the door
Me, I won't even know what they all
stand for.

He, will go on about stress,
metaphors and meter
Me, I just won't have a clue,

the only stress I know owt about
is the stress I'm living through

I'd tried to tell myself he's just
a man, not a cannibal or owt like
that
but my mind thinks I'm kidding myself
and it won't believe the chat.

My fears nearly beyond belief,
but when tomorrow's yesterday
it'll be a blessed relief.

Joan Peebles

SAINT BEDE'S
(Dedicated to Saint Bede's Church, Bedlington)

When God looks on the world today
He must be sad indeed
To see so many people
Not following his lead
To be good and kind and generous
To all our fellow man
Instead we turn our backs
We don't help them when we can

We say peace be with you
And shake them by the hand
But outside church we change
Into a very different band
With no time for people
To show them that we care
We turn into snobs
And stick our noses in the air

It costs nothing to say 'Hello'
And give a friendly smile
To everyone we meet
And it makes life more worthwhile
So come on all parishioners
Let us make a start today
To be nicer to all people
That we meet along life's way

The old folk, the young and middle group too
Let us all pull together and see this job through
To be kind to all people and help them in their needs
And God will smile down and say
      'Well done Saint Bede's'

S A Shippen

WALLSEND CRANES

The cranes are hungry on the Tyne
In obelisked sky line
Whetted appetites river born
Crops are empty at chilly dawn

Cranes upraised to dizzy heights
Vainly straining uprights
Against the chain, silent as the men
Who rally here again and again

Pigeons wheel around the clock
Strangely silent like the dock
Birdlike viewing the silent Tyne's
Dinosauric sky-lines

Silence holds the cranes in bondage
Statuesque at their moorage
Dinosaurs of modern birth
Jurassic time-served here on earth

The cranes are dying on the Tyne
In cloud capped obelisk design
Starved of sustenance
Sublime in dominance

Rope and pulley, block and tackle
Merely serve as erected shackle
To vigilantly posturing past
Now nailed firmly to the mast.

Georgina Francis McKellar

AGE CONCERN

Old age gives you time to think
Of events well past, men gone before.
The tales of wars and old folklore
But ones with which we love to link.
Beamish now recalls those ghosts
Of miner's feet, the trams, the steel.
But Consett's gone - and now the seal
On ships - and fish along these coasts.

There is a great change in morals we say,
(though readers of Cookson's Lords and their maids!)
But young ones sincerely say that those days
are now in the open - not hidden away!

We sit in our chairs, reflecting the past,
The Milburns, the Charltons, Fred Trueman, the Great.
How times have moved on - we're so out of date.
It's Keegan, the Magpies, hoisting the mast.

Those spans of five bridges over the Tyne.
Monumental reminders of sheer guts and sweat.
'Twas awa the lads then, *still* now, you can bet
Us Geordies *will* fight to stop a decline.
So old industries gone, replaced by the new.
Computers, Jap cars, Metro-centre and all.
'They'll never take off' are words we recall.
Now, pride of the nation and beat Europe too!

But hey there, it's time for jog and aerobics.
Get out of our chairs to take part in classes.
There's pensioners' lunches and chat with the lassies.
Then Latin-American - *and* French for specifics!

Which all goes to show that age is a thought
to get rid of at once before we all come to nought.

Pauline Hearnden

MARKET RESEARCH POEM

Excuse me, madam, sir,
just a moment of your time.
Are you into modern poetry?
Do you prefer free verse to rhyme?

How often do you read it?
On average twice a week?
Do you get a buzz from the language
or study the technique?

Which brand of poet is your usual read?
McNeice is back in vogue,
Then there's Auden, Lowell, Stevie Smith,
Hughes, Betjeman and Logue.

Or is something lighter to your taste?
Like Mitchell or McGough?
The New Generation lot are popular,
although they turn me off!

Going back to poetry itself
would you say its major strength
was tightness and good scansion
and making sure the last line of each verse was of a suitable
and appropriate content in meaning and in length?

Thank you for answering our questions.
It's now time that we came clean.
You've qualified for a subscription
to our literary magazine!

Graham C Brown

THE POP GROUP

We're one of those groups, with lots of long hair
And fans we blast into submission
With one of those names that doesn't make sense
Like the date, or price of admission
We smash our equipment with well defined rage,
Whenever we're paid to appear on the stage
But if you should see us looking pensive,
It's because these tantrums are proving expensive,
We love our agent, at times think it funny -
That he always takes home most of our money,
But we don't begrudge it, a good agent pays,
We've been in show business nearly six days!

Denny Boyce

FREEWAY?

There is no toll to be paid
On Britain's motorways they say
Yet, I know a dreadful toll
Is paid upon them every day

No cash involved, but richer far
Sweet life itself is given
May every innocent victim
Be recompensed in Heaven.

A distraught wife, hysterically waving
Runs near husband, who's sadly past saving
Grass-propped by the roadside
He vomits blood
Unaware of road-strewn garments
That should have been
Destined for holiday beaches.

God, I hope you're there!

A grandma lies still
By the side of a car
She intended, poor soul
To be travelling far
Oh, may her journey
Be straight to a star.

God, *I pray that you're there*!

Vera Sykes

UNTITLED

War - such a short word, three letters,
      but such consequences
Devastation, hunger, injury, pain
Bewildered children, elderly and infirm, relatives
      desperate and scared.
These children, orphaned by one single blow -
      because of someone's ideal for a better world.

Stately buildings, pointing tall and proud to the sky
      reduced to dust
Time, space, heritage, history, years of toil by these
      same men's hands
Those seeking the ideal world
Creating destruction of that not ours to destroy
A world only loaned to us for a short while - our life.

Eyes staring blankly to the sky - never seeing -
Fear still etched on their faces - young faces, old too soon
The noise of battle still ringing in their ears.
Twisted and mutilated bodies, left to die in no-man's land.
They have died . . . captor and captive, bodies entwined in death
      though not in life
Sons, husbands, fathers - crying wives and children - what
      of their future?
Who is the victor? - War never claims a winner.

Young souls trapped in the dark earth for ever
None able to feel the heat of the sun - view the blue of the sky
Nameless plots with nameless markers - remembered only in the
      hearts of others.

Stark white crosses in an empty field
Spilled blood transformed into crimson poppies -
      beauty not of the men's hands
The silence of eternal peace - a resting place -
The last post for brave and fearless men.

Carol Cobbledick

NON-EXPRESS, OK!

Leaving the station
and over the bridge,
people and ironwork
high on a ridge;
but -
fog on the line
train very late,
absence of driver
'You'll have to wait!'

Quick change at Durham,
bus driver related
to all Minstrels Wandering
(journey ill-fated);
finally getting there
hurry and scurry,
up to the hill-top
of Roger de Ferry!

Tracey Taylor

UNDER THE SURFACE

Take a deeper look into this town.
Stare into its waters, can you see all the way down,
Don't just peer at the surface all clear and calm,
It's the things down below that will cause alarm.

Down in the depths of its dimly lit streets,
Lurk differing creatures consisting of liars and cheats,
Don't venture out at night, keep behind closed doors,
The ones who didn't heed the warnings still carry nasty scars.

Some wander around lost in their own pathetic world,
Never getting back to reality, for them no future will unfold,
Engulfed in a cloud of smoke from a stiffening joint,
Others speed it up with a jab, but I can't see the point.

The old and vulnerable cower in the darkness,
Hardly seeing the light of day, their lives a complete mess,
Preyed on by sharks taking what little they own,
Then left to piranhas, chewed right down to the bone.

Did you see under the surface, it's not so clear down there,
The water's too murky, you'd better come up for air,
The bottom's been disturbed, it's now all cloudy and brown,
It's too late for the creatures now, they've been left to drown.

Andrew Curran

LOOK AND LISTEN

Listen to the barley field
Whispering in the wind
Look and see the ripples
As if some mighty hand
Approving of the sea of green
Turning soon to gold
Touched with caressing fingers
A hand time cannot hold
The hand of our creator true
The same God who
Made me and you

Listen to the voice of God
Across the barley stalks
He's whispering beloved one
See, my creation talks
It tells my glory
Shows my care
My greatness
I am always there

J Facchini

SMALL POTATOES

Mum and I, digging potatoes
at the bottom of our wilderness garden
laughing like drains as she makes me
throw stones in the bucket to con
the neighbours that the spuds are huge
not the sweet small ovals that we always found,
no matter what she planted.

The things you grew were small -
carrots like babies' fingers, petit pois,
cherry tomatoes, little gems -
and we three, none of us over five six
in spite of stews and chops, rosehip syrup
and cod liver oil.

You dreamed our giant destinies,
Nobel prizes, towering intellects,
talents of immense proportions.
But we were average - how to disguise
our failure to thrive?

Things about you: you always wanted more
than you got, so nothing was enough.
You couldn't see that small was often lovely
perfect in its way, so sometimes
we felt we failed you.

You, mum, bent over the rich Welland earth
Bum in the air, sly as a barrel of monkeys
Your freckled hands finding only fool's gold.

Jo Colley

THIS IS MY LIFE

Saturday was ordinary, like any other day.
I washed the dirty dishes and put them all away.
Then I prepared the dinner, steak and Yorkshire pud,
Put in a load of washing. Things were going good.
I switched on the radio, to listen to a song,
Decided I would iron, that's when things went wrong.
The blooming iron blew a fuse and what a bang it made,
The flex went up in flames, but my wrist was in the way.
I spent the next hour tending to my burn
My arms and legs were shaking and my stomach started to churn.
Monday came around, my appointment at the school,
Listening how our Alan was always being a fool.
before I left the school, a bill for me to pay,
£24 for window Alan broke the other day.
Walking back home my feet were hurting so,
My arm was really stinging, then it started to bleeding snow.
I went to bed at night, tired and worn out.
Tomorrow is another day, things might just go right.
But alas it was not to be, I got another shock,
Someone's stolen David's car, what rotten bloody luck.
These things to me are trivial,
You maybe think I'm thick.
The only time I worry is if my family's sick.

Margaret Atkinson

MY DAD

My dad is a happy man
not always I might add.
He can be sad and grumpy
when everything is going bad.

My dad is a witty man.
If anyone can make you laugh, he can!
He takes life in one big stride.
He holds his head high with pride.

His inventions keep everyone amused.
Every nut and screw is always re-used.
He is well know for fixing when
something has gone wrong.
He's always there with a hammer or wire,
ready to fix a Hi-fi or even a tyre!

He also has an amazing garage,
anything you need will be here.
My dad knows where everything is
even spiders give him no fear!
I wouldn't change him for anything
you see, because my dad is very
Special to me!

Lucy Hindmarch (13)

CLOUD OF TEARS

Floating gently across the sky
Gently weeping Oh! But why?
Silvery grey, gliding - but lost.
Drifting away - but at what cost?

Do they know where they are going,
Is the heart beating or slowing?
Is there still a warm glow -
We are not sure, we do not know.

Weeping down upon the soil
Joining the rivers in turmoil,
Clouds burst with expressive passion
Crashing down in unruly fashion
Churning the ground to a sodden pulp.
The earth then takes in a massive gulp
Then peace arrives and stills the air
Moving gently and with extreme care,
Returning life once more to calm
Now removing all panic and alarm.

Only solitude and silence now remain.
Golden shadows peep out across the plain.
The cloud of tears now have died.
For they are gone far and wide.

Soft and gentle clouds appear
No more thundering do we hear.
What did it mean? What did it teach?
Don't chase clouds - they're out of reach!

Jane Webber

DAD

Where are you where have you gone?
I know I cannot see you, yet I can feel you with me.
You didn't say goodbye, farewell or 'so long'.
You weren't to know, how could you.
This last farewell sneaks upon us.
It waits in the wings until we are not looking.
Do we have time to prepare? No.
Time to share our last hugs and kisses.
You weren't given that time.
Maybe it would have been too much to bear.
Even now I cannot believe you have gone.
So much of my life shared with you.
That life you gave me.
So much has gone by that I wanted to show you,
To tell you, to share with you.
How do we comprehend a loss so great?
How do we deal with death?
Somehow we do.
I did.

I miss you Dad.

Carolyn Foggin

THE MOTH MAIDEN

A flicker to the powder streamed light.
One pure flash of delicacy, to settle.
Meshed as the wick of a scented candle.

Her falling dew-drops to tears of hue.
The flight of infectious rhythm.

The Moth Maiden blinks with tender velocity.
In my slowed wink of an eye, trying to
grasp the brief flutter.

Smooth tarnish frays to my fingers.
Blown out with the moon's cloak.
Framed of her horizon.
Blending with the ivory silk.
One lost moment of inspiration.

Silent pardon.
Her wings drift to some other
awaiting magnetic source of light.

Joanna Ashwell

MEANING AND INTERPRETATION II

Today,
I neglected to mark your absence,
Engraved in the wall,
Beneath your photograph.

I will not forget,
But I think I'm over you.

Aidan Moesby

IT'S IN THE BAG

I spotted a man with an Early Learning bag, drag his child across the road,
As the lights stuttered orange.
I saw Mrs Khan tiptoe past her own corner ship with four Tesco bags,
Flesh pot full.
At the car boot sale, the trader with the caterpillar eyebrows,
Bundled the dodgy toaster into a Principles carrier,
While the fortune teller wrapped her crystal ball in bubbles, and stored it
                                                                                      in a Next bag.
The singles night shopper bought choco-condoms, and hid them in his
                                                                                       Safeway bag
Under the chicken curry for two.
At the clinic, the sperm donor came with his top-shelf tabloids in a
                                                                                       Virgin bag.

From the Restawhile Retirement Home, I watched a dead person being
                                                                    carried out in a body bag.
The bag was plastic, brown, zipped like a document case,
But it bore no name.

Carolyn Brookes

UNSOLVED CRIME

A tiny celluloid doll
brown bobbed head
a moulded flower in her hair.
See her shrivel.

And Mona who was real,
splashed in dark headlines.
A small boy fishing
in the local pond
finds her wellington -
dismembered child,
unsolved crime.

And that bigger crime
darkening the sky.
The slow dawning of Chernobyl,
screen-glow in the corner of the room.
I remember a fiercely burning centre,
and tiny doll-like figures
trying to douse
something out of control.

And the slow dying - later.
Babies like broken dolls.

Mary Shiells

HEARTS AND MINDS

I searched my mind
Like a shipwreck
For survivors

Heavy grew my heart
Scouring the sands
For a sign

By the ruins of a city
Laid waste by
The plague

I came and I saw
And I conquered
My fear

Without food without water
Death was vanquished
With laughter

Crystal Indiankhana Candy

A DAY OUT

The weather seemed quite bright, so I thought the time was right
To spend a happy day down on the beach.
I packed a flask of tea and a snack in a haversack on my back
And for my pudding I took a lovely juicy peach.

The ride on the crowded train was exciting, tho' a strain,
I was lucky to find myself a seat.
It was full of kids and mums looking for places to park their bums
And in their rush they trampled on my feet.

Well, I arrived there safe and sound, but the first thing that I found
Was, there wasn't any spaces on the sands,
A million bodies laid about *and* the blooming tide was out
So the matter was completely out my hands.

I thought the best thing I could do was to sit and have a chew
'Cos the hunger pangs were rattling in my tum,
I found an empty seat, enjoyed my peach so sweet,
Then the wasps decided *they* should join the fun.

So I made a quick retreat, gave up all attempts to eat
And hurried along the mile-long esplanade.
I dodged between the masses, decked in lotions and sun-glasses,
And my way back to the station I soon made.

While sitting on the train, returning home again,
I felt about as miserable as could be,
Then, much to my delight, I caught a flash of brilliant light,
As from the window I could actually see the sea!

With all the time and cash I spent on my one day dash,
I realised that it was not for me.
After all that's said and done; it's really much more fun,
Watching holiday progs at home, on my TV . . .

Olive Cartwright

BEATLES FOR SALE - AGAIN!

Beatles for Sale came out in '64, but here
we are 30 years later with the fans begging for
more

Martin their mentor trawled through the BBC
archives and emerged with a mass of classic cuts -
Light Programme *Lives*.

The raw enthusiasm of unsullied youth, who
could want more? Who need the Rolling Stones
when we've got the Fab Four!

Twenty-five years ago they called it a day,
but their music lives on - vinyl, cassette, CD,
whatever you want to play

A new single is out so those that weren't
born can revel in the sound that rocked the world
from Brazil to the Mountains of Mourne!

Coming from an Age of Innocence long gone by,
it's a welcome retreat from today's cynical and
knowing pop girl and guy

Ken Jackson

WATCHING TOM PLAYING THE PIANO

Sunlit windows
light up the piano,
and you, play. Hard
to express the essence
of the occasion,

a fervent adrenaline rush
provoked by your hesitant
keyboard movements,
your innocence overwhelms
all but the most

cynical in me. Trepidation
over quality buried
by the clear, unique
unforgettable emotional
implosion I remember.

Robert Mills

ONCE IN A WHILE

I welcome solitude
The chance to unwind,
From the daily pressures
Total peace of mind.

To have time to myself
Daydream if I wish,
To close my eyes and drift
Into a state of bliss.

Nice thoughts are in my head
As I reminisce,
Of bygone days and friends
Family I miss.

Contentedness I feel
Music fills my ears,
Relaxes me within
Drives away my fears.

Writing gives me pleasure
Letters, prose or poem,
Pictures are a calmer
And plants around my home.

Exploring a Thesaurus
Lose myself in words,
Nature's gifts I marvel
Flowers, trees and birds.

Peace and quiet are soothing
They also play a part,
All these things are pleasing
To my eye and heart.

Jean Cumbor

THE CANDLE FLAME

A sun hung in the empty sky, a dead sea flowed below,
An empty town stood witness to a people long ago.
Once there had been a future, a way ahead for all,
But now disease had taken those who had survived the wars.
The chemicals in weed sown ground, the thick smog in the air,
The dead plants and trees around the World - pollution everywhere.
Why couldn't man just get it right, why couldn't he just try,
To live in peace with nature like the birds do with the sky.
But all through time he got it wrong and never got it right,
The end came with a whimper, a fading candle in the night.

Paul Sanders

A MOVING STORY

When I was a kid I loved empty rooms
where useful things were kept and forgotten
and dust, like Sherlock's clever traps, kept
a record of who'd been in, and when.

Now I own empty rooms. Six of them.
The useful things have gone with the seller
and what remains are dints in the carpets
grey halos round the switches and sockets
hair, toenail clippings.

I know who's been in and they're glad to be out.
Now, I have to fill it and wait, forget where
I put this or that, and let dust settle.

Tim Butler

VOYAGE TO THE STARS

I am a voyager
Come with me on a journey into space.
In my vessel of the skies we will travel
through the galaxies.

First stop - the moon.
The mad, mysterious moon.
Moon of romance.

Then to the Milky Way.
We will ride the Plough.
Listen to the grumbling of The Great Bear
Say hello to The Seven Sisters.

Let us circle the heavens
and orbit other planets . . .
Mars, Venus, Uranus
and Neptune.

We are immortal travellers in time
with worlds at our feet.
We will be voyagers together.
Come with me . . .
Now.

Sara Newby

PAINTING

Palette, key to summer land
realm of make-believe
a land where flowers never fade
and children never leave

Misty, smudgy, painted land
where washes subtle shade
as indistinct a fairy land
within a forest glade

The creatures held in this small place
an instant caught in time
a watching silence in their eyes
light captured eyes which shine

This insubstantial paper world
painted, illusive scene
time for a fleeting moment stayed
thought of what might have been?

If power blind eyes could only see
if greed would stay its hand
a dreaming world forever free
we could live the way God planned.

Joy Scarr

THE MAN

Was it only a few years ago?
When I did not really know
How to speak my mind
In affairs of the heart

Now those times have gone
And as the years roll on
The words I need to find
Don't leave me torn apart

Calmness has returned again
Like a long lost friend
And though I lose sleep
I don't worry much at all

I get the feeling into sight
No matter if it's day or night
Some things you just don't keep
My head's stopped banging on the wall . . .

It used to be -
'30 pushing 40'
But now 50 lies ahead
Not too far in the distance

It used to be -
'I'm losing the race, not keeping pace'
But now I feel
I understand my circumstance

Maybe I always did
Maybe I always will
And so I see the man inside
And in him I now confide

He never left
He only waited for -
A little self-respect . . .

Bernard Harry Reay

DREAMS

'And so to bed,' the old man said,
'it's time to dream. I shall be led
down paths of wonder, lands anew,
fantasies and old things too.'

The magic of subconscious mind
is not like any other kind.
In waking hours the things we keep
locked in there are released in sleep.

The images we then can see
are wondrous but sometimes can be
quite frightening, but we mustn't fuss,
we know they really can't harm us.

So while awake we must beware
of images we store in there,
for waiting just to be released
could be the most horrific beast.

The darkness falls - the moonlight beams.
And so to sleep - perchance to dream.

M Hulse

THE REAPER'S TALES

I took their lives, I made them bones
I ignore their bribes, their pleas, their moans
My job is simple, I am to collect
I'm the bastard of bastards, I deserve no respect
I'm God's hated messenger, the Devil's cohort
I'm the one they all blame, when a life is cut short
But still if you're willing to give it a try
I'll beat you at anything, and claim your last sigh
I am no respecter of race, age or health
The rich will fall too, regardless of wealth
The millionaires, the destitute, all come to me
I'm the great equaliser, your soul's all I see
Before the stairway to heaven, or highway to hell
You'll have to face me, and I don't look so well
My face is of bone, my scythe harvests all
My hourglass is empty, and my cloak ends life's call
Maybe you'll see me, at the death-bed of friends
But look into my face, and that's where it ends
I have no prejudice, I can take one or more
I'll take the killers, like I took their victims before
Suicides flock to me, their lives seem all messed
But if life has no guarantees, haven't they guessed?
The Beyond is no better, troubles only get deeper
You're wheat in the wind, and I'm the Grim Reaper.

Peter Lennox (16)

THROUGH A GLASS DARKLY

In a time of blunted sensibility,
Do we acknowledge we are still aware of them?
I mean those moments of vision,
Reminding us all too rarely
That whenever we look at the world,
We are not simply looking at it
But seeing it for perhaps the first time.

Forgetting all too often that seeing and looking
Are not, nor can be, the same thing,
We look idly at the humble dandelion -
Taraxacum Officinale -
And take our act of looking
For an act of seeing
And think we see a weed.

But what is a weed, essentially?
The word's familiar of course,
But words are labels, nothing more.
So what do I see when I look at the world
Through eyes that lack vision?
Aware of the shadow, I never see the substance.

But there are moments, gladsome, marvellous,
When it's as if the entire world
With a blink of an eyelid
Had been renewed, remade,
And I'm seeing it clearly
For the first time
In the heart of a flower.

Frank Knaggs

OLD DAYS OF SUMMER'S YIELD

Golden is the corn shimmering in the breeze
intermingled in the fields are poppies
Flaunting their scarletness as if to
prove the brevity of their duress
Memories of long sunlit summers
long long days dipping into the night
Cider sweet and strong, or ginger
beer babies lined up on the pantry floor
Home-made bread what an aroma
issuing forth from every cottage door
Market days, barrows laden with
fruits of the earth abounding for all
to choose, strawberries, pears and
bilberries to stain mouths quite purple
Hurry them home for jam to be made
together with lemon curd or honey
What a feast tea time used to be
Doorsteps of bread butter and cheese
Our palates sure to please
no instant meals of microwave flavour
but good wholesome food for all to savour

M L Gabriele

THE ADULT DINOSAUR

The pleasure of childhood has been ghosted away
All playgrounds empty; no children play.
No swings are squeaking, no sound to say
A tombstone of leisure is left to decay

Where are the old days of carefree fun?
Footballs and skipping ropes, children run.
Away with their innocence out into the sun
But rain stops play and they've nowhere to run

So they all stand still like lambs to the slaughter
As the politics of power plot a childhood take over.
The government elect in their wisdom select
Instead of playtime, computer run grey time.
Where an adult dinosaur raises its head and
Says 'My gift to our youth is life's worries instead.'

Patrick Humble

THINK 'N' ACT

In ninety four an annual appraisal
meditation, philosophy and melancholy
finally, all considered.
Many more worse off, we speak, see and hear
Whatever? A positive reverie

In ninety five the thunder clapped
more fiercely, nerves are shot
Where have all the birds gone?
Did you really say that? My face awry, tongue flailing
Watch me for my answer

Confused and darkness closing, but
'Thank you' surgeons, all is lifted
Battles fought but not all won, no victory
in glorious summer
Pain like October beckons unceasingly, kill my will

Twelve months scarred, scared, future melancholy
What faith? He has deserted me
Reflections, being fair, considered, not yet lost
Duty draws me back to labour on
Actions spur me, no more reverie.

Jean Horsham

OLD ROVER

The old dog lies there scratching
Contentment you can see.
Chasing the itches all around
Grunting, happily.

But underneath the forest of hairs
On Rover's itching rump.
A group of unhappy residents
Complain about this dump.

The leader stands there shouting,
'We'll give him no release'
And all the residents agree
'Tonight he'll get no peace.'

So they all got together
A party was in store.
Dancing, singing and eating
Poor Rover he'd be sore.

The party is all over
And everyone's asleep
Poor Rover lies exhausted
Sick of his itching heap.

Sylvia M Thompson

THE WIND

A clear chilly stranger,
That nobody knows.
Yet the rattling clearness,
Hides a mischievous pose.

The battling adventure,
Forced on through the leaves,
Entrance and exit
That no-one believes.

Yet I move onwards still,
A slowing down spill.
To calm breeze I tire
Gentle . . . stop . . . then expire.

Stephen Grant (10)

MY CHILDREN

Even though I see you every week
Since your Mum and I separated months ago
When we meet I find it hard to speak
Dear Timothy and Mollie how I miss you both so

I'm here alone and you are over there
When we meet you kiss me and call me Dad
Only once in seven days can I show you I care
I love you both so very much it makes me sad

Will you still love me in the years ahead
Will I still be *Dad* even when I'm dead
Please don't forget me
Please don't forget me.

Peter White

THE SILVER SWAN

Upon a silent silver stream,
beautiful and all serene
swims The Silver Swan of Bowes.
Keeping what secrets, no-one knows?

No crust of bread upon her dish, for,
she sups on little silver fish.
No breeze ruffles those feathers, so fine,
but a shaft of moonlight makes them shine.

A spell around you she weaves,
as you watch her,
by a bank of silver leaves,
beautiful and all serene
swimming upon a silent silver stream.

Angela Fishwick

MEMORIES OF THE SEASIDE

The tang of salt, the sound of waves,
the sand, the sun, the sea,
Candy floss on wooden sticks,
brings memories to me.

Children clutching buckets,
mothers heave and sigh,
grandmas in their deck chairs,
watching folk go by.

The passing round of sandwiches
soggy, full of grit.
Lemonade that's warm and flat,
we didn't mind a bit.

The smell of chips and vinegar,
the ice cream sellers cry,
seagulls soar above the cliffs,
against a clear blue sky.

The sound of fairground roundabouts,
of people having fun,
the sight of knotted handkerchiefs,
protected from the sun.

The sun on the horizon,
across a calm blue sea,
weary folk all homeward bound
brings memories to me

Cathy Thomas

RED

The sweet aroma of rosé wine floating on waves of perfumed indulgence pounds the shore of tingling anticipation.

Seductive skirts of swirling scarlet beckon.

Blades of hardened steel honed to razor sharp precision gouge yielding flesh, shattering bone, shooting spurts of pressurised spray into jets of fine crimson mist.

Spasms of twitching flesh sway and list
The watching crowd look; pissed.

Boiling bubbles of blood spill over arena floor.
Applause
The strutting Matador.

Jim Gardiner

IAN

There is still an empty place at the table,
There is still an empty chair in the room,
There is still a card that I miss sending,
There is a present that I haven't bought.

The laughter from a loving friend is silent,
The fight for the bathroom doesn't come,
The racing down the stairs to be first in the room
And the fourth pile of presents has all gone.

Christmas has changed so very much,
Since God took you to be with him,
It has lost that special glow of magic,
The one that followed you into any room.

There is an awful aching in my heart,
There is a loneliness that I can't shake off,
There is a missing you that never leaves us Ian,
And a wishing you were here that never goes.

May your Christmas bring you peace,
Whilst your memory gives us love,
And may the kisses that I send to you,
Reach you through God above.

J Lunn

PEACE AND LOVE

Peace is watching a flower's petals open.
Watching ripples on the sea.
Peace is listening to bird song.
Being with the ones you love.
Peace is saying thank you to God..
For your children's health - happiness.
But war is watching the land being torn apart.
The waters filled with blood - hate.
Wild life killed through fires - guns.
War is your loved one's taking from you.
You fear for your children's lives.
War is when you ask God why.
And pray you lived in a land
Where everyone didn't have to die.

V Wood

QUESTIONS AND ANSWERS

'What did you do in the war dad?'
My son, he asked one day,
'Did you fight the nasty Germans?
Or the Japs in Mandalay?

Did you fly a fighter aircraft?
Or sail the ocean blue?
Oh come on dad please tell me,
Please tell me, tell me do.'

I sat and thought some minutes,
Before I raised my head,
And thought of all my comrades,
Long forgotten, maybe dead.

I pondered on his questions,
And knew that it would be,
The truth, and nothing but the truth,
My son would get from me.

'I did my bit,' I answered,
And looked him in the eye,
'They put me in the army,
A corporal there was I.

To serve my King and country,
I did my very best,
To honour the old regiment,
And win medals for my chest.

But as for killing anyone,
Though many say I tried,
As a cook I served at Catterick,
Thousands suffered, but none died.'

G Richardson

DARK SECRET

Soft and velvety
It brushes my face,
Catching my cheek
It leaves a slight trace.

Behind me now,
The beating of the wings,
Piercingly a shriek,
In the still night rings.

Over my foot
With just a slight pause,
A scurrying creature,
With razor sharp claws.

A muffling sound
In the sultry heat,
The champing of jaws,
then hurrying feet.

Strands of silk,
Too fine to see,
A prisoner released
Unknown to me.

Eyes trying to see
Through the darkest of night,
No stars in the sky,
No moon's light.

Dew comes from where?
The grass is all wet,
This is yet another,
Of the night's dark secrets.

Joan Jemson

BETRAYAL

Dark pools beneath the leafy canopy
Moving slowly with the orb of time.
Two lovers, limbs entwined in ecstasy,
Whisp'ring words of love, their thoughts sublime.

The lowering clouds approach and with them, death,
In form of outraged man intent on harm.
His world collapsing with each heavy step
His heated rage cooling to chilling calm.

A chance remark, a smile, a sidelong glance,
A huddled group gone quiet on approach
Conveyed a message to him, quite by chance
Of treachery by those he loved the most.

His friend, with whom he toiled in daily grind
And who was always there in times of strife
The other, who had long ensnared his heart
On whom he had bestowed the title, *wife*.

He saw them lying there serene and still
His heart rending in two, the searing pain
He felt the metal, hard and strangely chill
Against his shaking hand as it took aim.

Two shots,
        A silence,
        Then a searing cry
Rose up.
        Another shot, and all was still.
The silent witness reaching to the sky
Its branches swaying on that sombre hill.

Crimson pools beneath the canopy
With scarlet fingers spreading in the sun
Itself becoming scarlet as it sets
On tragedy, where once there was pure love.

E Wilson

DAFFODILS

A green shoot springs up from the earth
It is alive it has rebirth,
In its bulb still, it lies in wait
For the season, it springs into being
We can then view, forever seeing
As taller and stronger the leaves rise up high
Then out of the centre springs the flower in bud
Then pushes its petals out, a golden flood,
A daffodil springs forth this day
Its golden trumpet rises to say
This is spring, this is spring, I came to shout,
Lots of golden trumpets now sway in the breeze
All reaching up to look at the sun
A brilliant sight in the noonday sun,
The green and the yellow, how they blend together
For our earthly pleasure it seems to last forever
A carpet of daffodils that sway in the breeze
Brings us so much pleasure, that we long to please,
We plant them, the bulb, so still and brown
As down in the earth they lie so still
Collecting nourishment their bulb to fill,
But O, the pleasure that we all see
is the golden trumpets that open, to say
It is spring, it is spring, I am here today
I will gladden your garden in gold
Look this way, do not hurry past
I came to say, watch me, I am here to say
For I came to give you pleasure
On this springlike day.

Lillian R Gelder

WFTB

When next you visit your GP
And I hope it isn't too soon
Just be prepared for a long wait
Maybe from 9 till noon

There's such a lot of 'flu about
Of bugs there is a spate
But something's sweeping through the land
At epidemic rate

It's not your heart and not your chest
Not even mild bronchitis
Nor gall stones, jaundice or a stroke
Nor our old friend arthritis

It's got a name, WFTB
Quite new to the profession
But we've all got it old or young
You get it with concession

And if you're wondering what it is,
This cursed WFTB,
You all know all about it,
Just take a tip from me.

The GP doesn't need to use
His shiny stethoscope,
He'll shake his head and murmur low,
'My dear there is no hope.'

Because we're stuck with this complaint,
We cannot make a fuss,
Do you know what these four letters mean
It's *Waiting For The Bus.*

Eleanor Pace

MEN WITHOUT THEIR BOOTS

We had the docks the steel and the mines
All have gone, it's a shame and a crime
I don't want to sound terrible or to be mean
But people don't want job clubs or a scheme
there was plenty to do at the Tyne
A man held his head up and could say 'That is mine'

Nothing new comes in our home, I'm down to my *last pair of socks*
    How I wish I could turn back the clocks
    What else has to go?
    Nothing left for us to show
Our shops are closing 1-2-3-4 or more
Before long I won't need to open my door

You could hear men in working boots walking down the path
Nothing do I hear, nothing does anyone have
    Nothing left for us on the Tyne
    Just the dole for everyone to sign.

V Robson

WINTER

Winter is great with lots of fun in
Snow and hail stone
Scarves, coats, and little hats
Also with gloves to match
Winter clouds snow and fog
It's fun playing out with my little dog
All the leaves are gone from the trees
Our park pond is starting to freeze
Soon I'm indoors all nice and warm
Everything's so quiet and calm.

Gemma Quinn (11)

INTO TOMORROW

Electric lights are fading
Leaving shadows on the earth
Is this the end of everything
Or just technology's birth?

Hearts are just like robots
Cold and made of steel
Nobody seems to care any more
And love just isn't real.

Brainwashed into believing
Computers can take control
But they don't have feelings
Or a sentimental soul.

Skyscrapers looming over us
And no fauna to be seen
Animals dying to extinction
What does the future mean?

It's in the land of tomorrow
Where dreams are built on lies
And the planet we once knew
Will die before our eyes.

Marie Ness

MEDITATION

The light from the heavens streams down from the skies, to enlighten the heart and make the soul rise. To blend in reunion with God three in One. Divine love forever when God's will is done.
The soul reaches up to our Father above, where He moulds it with His perfect love. Sharing forever His gifts given free, harmonious with music for you and me.
Rainbows surround us with colours from high, when after a shower we gaze at the sky. Love forever awaits thee if only we'd open our eyes, hearts and see that God is with us, within you and me.

Brenda Norman

HOLIDAYS

Some British people have a strange habit of going abroad each year
And turning up their nose at those who prefer to stay here,
As soon as they are off the plane they search for a British-type pub
And some lovely traditional fish and chips or steak and kidney pud

They burn themselves red raw as they laze beside the pool
With their multi-coloured shorts and sandals on they look such a fool
They can't understand the currency, and the foreign food makes them ill
And for a decent pint of beer, I'm sure they could kill

But they are just a clique and always follow the crowd
They seem to think a holiday in Britain simply cannot be allowed
I prefer to spend my holiday in this green and pleasant land
Instead of struggling to find a space on some crowded foreign sand.

Sue Pine

SISTERS

Louise was a picture with love on her face
When her sister Ashley joined the human race
She was not astounded after talks with her mummy
That Ashley had grown inside her mum's tummy
Isn't this a grand reason to have truth unfold
Beats stork delivery as some kids are told
Even better than babies found under a bush
Such a super occasion should not be hush hush.

J S McKinney

THE MAGIC OF WINTER

There is magic all around us
Sparkling crystals everywhere
And each and every window pane
Has a picture designed with care.

The dew has been turned into diamonds,
The water to shimmering ice,
The trees are aglow with glistening coats
As if the magic had touched them twice.

Now the one who created these changes
Moves silently unseen
And when you see the beauty of winter
You will know that Jack Frost has been.

D Cowan

BROKEN
(For Lee)

A child wanders across the city,
Something stirs
There it strikes
A stab of hate put paid to us,
All dies here.
Your friend lives beneath the sea,
He takes your hand,
Do you believe?
A banished infant screams for me,
I cannot help
I can deceive.
Lay your sweet head upon a bench of bramble
Or shards of glass
So you may bleed.
There is no one to protect you
To chase away the demons
Who must catch you,
Then you are lost.

Beneath the shining blue ocean
That friend awaits
Clutching a teddy bear,
But he is too late.

Shawn W Le Gard

EVERY TOY HAS ITS DAY

As midnight strikes, the toy-box stirs,
The toys' day's just begun.
They all come out, and look about.
They're going to have some fun!
Soldiers march and spaceships fly,
A football bounces low, then high.
Books open up and read themselves
Then jump right back upon the shelves.
The rocking horse swings to and fro.
The dolls' house lights begin to glow.
A clown looks down with utter glee
As Teddy Bears have picnic tea.

A shaft of moonlight lights the scene.
A child is fast asleep.
He dreams of toys that play like boys.
If only he could peep!

The music-box begins to play
And dancing dolls begin to sway.
A toy train chugs around the track.
It pauses . . . then it comes right back.

As morning breaks, and sun arises
The boy wakes up to some surprises.
'I didn't leave that spaceship there . . .
Has it been flying through the air?
My dream came true
The toys *do* play.
Or did I forget
To put them away?'

Eileen Potts

ARRIVAL

Imagine yourself as an alien being,
Sent to explore planet earth,
Your task is to study the life forms upon it,
And decide what its value is worth.

Choose your disguise, and method of study,
And how long you wish to remain,
But it won't really matter which viewpoint you take,
Your conclusions will be just the same.

Because it won't take you long to discover a trend,
Which permeates every existence,
Leaving its mark on all that it touches,
With an incomprehensible persistence!

No matter which form you decide to adopt,
Quite soon, you'll feel the effects,
Of a species intent on adapting 'its' world,
To whatever design 'it' selects.

You'll observe that the planet survives with a balance,
Perfected by nature's own hand,
Yet this creature ignores these natural laws,
An anomaly you can't understand!

For this species appears to possess common-sense,
And yet, it would rather deploy
Its abilities on creating wide-spread destruction,
In a world that could bring it such joy!

Your appraisal's complete, you've observed all you need,
You must now send home your conclusions,
Could you live with the creatures inhabiting this planet?
If not - suggest your *exclusions*!

T M Rutherford

MY WORLD OF DREAMS

I stirred then moved into a dream, and from my couch I slowly rose,
Dressed was I in suit of cream, cravat of red, and yellow hose,
I walked on carpet trimmed with lace, on through a doorway carved in oak,
Staircase lit with golden grace, which led me down to gentle folk.

People that I did not know, were speaking words in fluent flow,
Soon I realised a literary crowd, whose pleasing words of verse allowed,
Poets too in rhythmic style, who thrilled the world with many a score,
Actors too who could beguile, spectators who in turn encore.

These people from way back in time, discussing scenes and deeds of yore,
Some in prose and some in rhyme, with words that last for evermore,
Maybe somehow, perhaps somewhere, we as spirits together share,
A verse or two from olden time, once again in prose and rhyme.

There I listened for quite a while, much like a visitor lost in time,
Wondered how to find my way, back to my couch of every day,
Staircase left without a sound, while I stood with trees around,
Stars and moon and nightingale, plus troop of players who did prevail,
To end this pleasurable dream, and lead me back from where I've been.

F P Collinson

CHANGING TIMES

We're told we're recovering from this demise,
That's gripped our City of late,
But when I watch our changing tides,
It's hard to believe that fate,
Where are those tall ships,
Which graced our deep river beds?
Or the rattle of rivet guns,
Welcomed noisily overhead,
Where are the other industries?
Like forges, glass and mine,
'Gone,' they say, sadly,
Through ever evolving times,
Redundancies have reached their peak,
Our men and boys look spent,
As they wait in line each week,
For dole money to pay their rent,
Despondency glooms ahead,
For the many, not for the few,
That are lucky to strive and spread,
Their wages that are repeatedly due,
Now they say that our elders,
Must look to the cost of their keep,
There's no money left in the coffers,
To spend their last days in peace,
When will it end, this gloom,
That's rife in our very midst?
Let's hope change comes real soon,
And we all get what we wish.

Ruth Hughes

VISION OF THE BLIND

I would like to see a field of green
Hedgerows with their gates between
Trees standing there stately and tall
A house, a garden, an old stone wall
I would like to see a field of corn
And watch the breaking of the dawn
See the sun rise overhead
While an old cock crows, 'Get out of bed'
I would like to see a babbling brook,
Pierce its waters with a searching look
While listening to its merry song
As through the meadows I wander on
I would like to gaze into the sky
Watch the clouds go scudding by
See the moon, the stars, the sun
Watch the sunset as day is done
I would like to see a bird in flight
Be able to tell the day from night
This is the hardest part I find
You! You can see! I! I am blind.

A Gormly

CHILDHOOD'S END?

Born kicking and screaming into this world
Guns blazing and flags unfurled
Ready to hit life head on
Unaware of future's scorn
Life's centre stage without a care
Rollercoasting at the fair
Real friends around were many
Sunny days two a penny
Heart's friend was only love
Absence of hate and push and shove
No raised voices, no need to shout
No darkness, despair or even doubt
No need for questions, just answers
Or given thought for half-hearted romances
So up front, we never lied
Felt no shame if we cried
We lived our life and let our love grow
Never had to put on a show
Did we really want to come this far?
Just to keep our memories in a jar
Can't we be the same again?
Release the world of this great pain
Survival takes on elevation
Hence the chaos of our nation
'Life' is the greatest test
Isn't it time we changed for the best?

Martin Kenneth Watson

INSANITY

Four walls all around me
padded and white,
When I scream
No one hears me.
Is it day or is it
Night?

My food is pushed through
a flap in the door
But how can I eat
When my head feels
Sore?

An end to this madness
An end to it all
I sit alone in the corner
Banging my head against
The wall.

Tania Marie Lowerson

THE HOUSE

The house on the hill
Is a wondrous sight
I walk by often with great delight
Ivy creeps over the wall
The old trees are beautifully tall
The garden pond with gnomes all around
The fish sunbathe and frogs abound
The children playing on the swings
Grown-ups having tea
While songbirds sing
Happiness spares no expense, you see,
The house on the hill
Belongs to me.

J B Wilkinson

DAY TRIP

We're going on a trip today
Mum says 'Somewhere I can play'
Dad's got the map and filled the car
We must be going very far.

Nature calls, so I tell Dad.
I don't know why that makes him mad
It's only the third time we've had to stop,
Twice for nature and once for the shop.

We've been in the car for twenty years
Dad's pulling out all his hairs.
'We're nearly there, not far to go'
Dad said that an hour ago.

'Never again' growls Dad aloud
I don't think he's very proud,
His little boy has made him swear,
But we're here now, so I don't care.

James W Harvey

AS A CLOUD

I wandered lonely, as a cloud
Of diesel fumes enveloped me ...
And all at once I couldn't breathe,
I couldn't think, I couldn't see!
Beside the road, across the bridge,
As I walked on to cross the ridge.

The day had started very well,
With sunshine glinting on my way,
And as I walked, I gloried in
The splendour of an autumn day
Until my path led by the roads
Complete with lorries and their loads.

And then it was my throat went dry,
My head was woozy, eyes did run,
The lorries and their deadly fumes
Had now deprived me of my fun.
I quickly changed direction, 'til
I breathed the air on Penshaw Hill.

I pondered on the days gone by
When walks were pleasure to enjoy,
Unspoilt by traffic and its noise
And other problems which annoy.
Walking on grass, beneath the trees
One could enjoy the morning breeze.

Anne Chisholm

THAT FEELING!

When certain people are around,
The air is filled with a wonderful sound,
You can sense it everywhere,
Even feel it in your hair,
You've got a wonderful feeling inside,
A feeling that you just can't hide,
You can see it, smell it,
Hear it, feel it, even taste it,
You never want to let them go,
And to them all your feelings show.

Lynne Blakelock (16)

FUTURISTIC THOUGHTS

I leave my underground home and step forth into
the fierce sunlight, shimmering umbrella in hand,
sun blocker streaked across a sunburned face.
Garments of silver cloth cover my cancerous sores,
as I stagger onward to fulfil my earthly duties.
Work is but a 'shadow of a shade', as computers work
in unison to make my brain idle and obsolete.
Feasting is now but a long, long memory as I devour
my colourful pills to sustain my hairless, puny body.
My allocated offspring sits at times, stupefied by
my programmed gadgets of enormous size. No time for
love of his parents - a concept he lost - nigh never
possessed. Is this the shape of things to come?

Alex Branthwaite

AFTER THE GOLD TARNISHED

I was standing in a circle of dancers, all singing in the snow,
Full of life, and hope and youth, those many years ago;
The dancers wheeled from left to right, and I fed from their fulsome glee,
The power pulsated deep inside, and something spoke to me.
I heard the angels' voices, they were whispering in the breeze,
And hints of the world's redemption were rustling through the trees.

I called to the longhaired children of the laughter and the light
And the lords of the snarling cycles that had wheeled in from the night,
I said 'Let's get the act together; I can hear the summoning bell,
Let's all project our spirits; we're making a raid on Hell.
We'll tie the Devil's tail in knots, and we'll let the damned go free;
We'll turn Hell into Heaven, so come and follow me!'

But the freaks all made excuses, so I went to Hell alone;
The Devil laughed, 'You and whose army?' so, ashamed, I set back home.
It's another generation must hear the summoning bell,
And it's heroes unknown and unthought of now must harrow the pits of Hell,
These days I wear a pinstriped suit, and I speculate in shares,
But I still recollect my honour. The freaks long ago lost theirs.

Eric Karlson

REMINISCENCE

My eyes are full of tears.
I cannot see.
What is this thing that's happened,
Between thee and me?

Where have all the days gone
I thought would last forever?
All there's left is memories
Of thee and me together.

The sun shone warm upon your face
Delight of my own heart;
How could I know, how could I tell,
How soon we'd have to part?

Those lazy, hazy summer days,
Were made for thee and me.
The charms I saw there, in your eyes,
Forever I will see.

There are marvellous pictures in my mind
No one can take away;
How I wish they all were real,
And I could be with you today.

Beauty's but a flower
That has not long to live.
You were blown away by the gentle breeze,
Yet, you had so much to give.

I have long days to remember
How you were plucked away from me;
I cannot live without you,
The flame is gone for thee, and me.

Doreen Baker

FAR AWAY YOU

Far away you
Hovering in the wind - treading on the ocean - the elusive rainbow.
I am lead - heavy-hearted - only knowing that I need you.
Far away you.

Far away you - golden - immortal
Balancing the world's glittering bubble on your palm.
I - clutching only a handful of ashes
Only knowing that I need you
Far away you.

Far away you.
Walking among the planets in flash-flickering starlight.
Dazzling you.
I rooted on earth - weighed down - only knowing that I need you.
Far away you.

E Stephens

YOU

The excitement
You cause
is something new.

The urgent calling of
Your skin,
Your movements,
the essence of You

is enough

to stir my bones
to shaky motion.
Involuntary reaction
beautiful
as the ocean

perhaps as deep.

The want
You show
is good an true.

The silky invite of
Your thighs,
Your mouth,
the smell of You

is enough

to vandalise words
I once began.
Speechless desire
mysterious
as this man

perhaps as real.

David E Golledge

FOR YOUR EYES ONLY

I'm a freelance Director and money's my game
I'm looking for a job on the gravy train.
As former Minister of a Public Utility
There's no doubting my special ability.
And for a seat on the Board and X grand a year
I'll work two days a week so it won't cost you dear
Your company's flotation should be equitable and fair
How about my know-how for the odd optional share?
My inside Knowledge at this present time
Is in your interest
and also in mine
All this talk of envy and greed
It's people like me the country need
A classless society all well and good
But it's us at the top that provide the food.
My credentials are impeccable you must agree
So I know you'll look favourable at this CV.

John Cougle

PAST THE LONGEST DAY

A cold dull day,
Mid summer,
Past the longest day.
Yet time feels . . .
Feels like it's standing still,
Swathed in grey dullness
Waiting for a change,
A break in the
Weather.
It will be soon.

An aura of premonition,
Not too far but distant seeing.
Something's out there
Through the dullness . . .
A blazing sun,
Blazing life,
To be taken in two hands.

Duncan A Smith

I AM

I am reality
I am non-existence
I am tender loving care
I am dislike and hatred
I am skin and I am bone
I am flesh and I am blood
I am your favourite dream
I am your worst nightmare
I am the past and future
I am now and I am never
I am nothing and something
I am life and I am death
I am all of these
I am many more
And if you want me
I am yours

Rebecca Minto

NORTH EAST MEMORIES

We can talk about the good old days recall a smile or tear
Within our close community that stands nearby the Wear,
Our chapels and our churches don't forget the Wheatsheaf clock
Many an eye has glanced its time as we stroll towards North Dock
The public houses visited it did not have to rain
A cry from the rag and bone man with his barrow in back lane
The pork shops and the fish shops where we often bought a bite
We got so much for pennies it filled one overnight
As daylight waned those gas lamps gave out a special glow
It really looked so magic against a fall of snow
Hammer noise from shipyards where men were building ships
The pride of all those workers of a launching down the slips
Bookies stood on corner and a betting slip would take
And if a horse did not come in some swore it was a fake
Women sit on doorsteps talking of what goes on
A drunken man then passes by his voice is in full song
He will be in for trouble when he reaches home
'Tis best to keep on walking safer for to roam
Bairns are playing along the street a nifty game of cricket
Took a loan of a dustbin lid perfect for a wicket
The clatter wakes a cat - a dog then chases it upstairs
The drunken man lying in the passage starts to say his prayers
Teatime at the table new oil baize smells so fresh
You are not allowed to have a meal until you wash
Sheep head broth and dumplings the in meal of the day
After you eat that lot you could ride the milky way
Saturday was the picture hall - Tom Mix he was a treat
The penny crush we called it for the baddies we stamped our feet
This canny place we lived in sad to say now gone
Monkwearmouth is a special place - forever to linger on.

Mary Robinson

MORNING SHADOWS

When night falls,
And breathes its scented shadow 'cross the land,
'Tis then I lay,
And turning thoughts within my mind,
Decide the outcome of the day.

Solutions sought,
Pass slowly through the stillness of the night,
Then fly! . . .
Like morning shadows,
Rude-awakened by the light.

Sleep comes,
All conscious thought takes wing,
'Tween bouts of sleep;
Low-whispered words;
And following;

Arrives the dawn,
The herald's call to start another day,
I rise from peaceful slumber,
Peaceful heaven,
Where I lay.

R Tose

LIFE IS CRUEL

I lie back and I close my eyes
My mind is full of wheres and whys
My heart is aching, full of pain
As I think of what I have to gain

I watch the children play their games
I hear them call each other names
What makes them think that it's alright
To push and shove and hit and fight?

So many things in this world seem wrong
Why can't we all get along?
What do I need to make them see
There's more to life than jealousy?

I often think of what I've seen
Why are people always mean?
Why do they live a life of lies
When every second another man dies?

I try and try but still can't see
The point of all this misery
People's reactions make me seethe
I close my eyes and cease to breathe.

H Bevan

A POEM OF DAYS IN MANY WAYS

What is a day when all around is grey?
Never again shall I gaze upon the sun
Never once more shall we meet
Sun shines but not for me.
Out here no fear
At home all alone
My thoughts turn
Swimming in my mind
Can I last without
Without the love you gave me?
Air is pure I need it too
What can I do when I do not have you?
Maybe I was wrong
Ten years long I wait
For distantly down the line
You wait for me outside Heaven's Gate.

Robert John Temple

THE SEA IS A SNAKE

The Sea is a snake coiling up into towering
waves and crashing
down on the sand with staggering impact.
I listen to it hissing and frothing while
slithering back down the beach.
And afterwards, sliding secretly towards me
to lick me with its many tongues.
With each attack it comes nearer
Struggling harder each time until exhausted,
Slipping back down in hiding it retreats again.

Mark Wilkinson

THE FASTEST SLATER IN THE WEST
(With apologies to Benny Hill)

You can hear his heel plates pound as they go flashing across the ground,
And the rattle of the wheels as they go round and round,
He is loaded up with ladders, stepboards and all the rest,
That's happy Harry the Slater and he drives the fastest handcart in the west.

The young lad there is the apprentice and he goes by the name of John,
He whistles at all the young girls, by gum he is a one,
Then there's Bob that handsome labourer whose judgement you can trust,
When it comes to picking horses his nap it is a must,
This trio go round all the houses, mending roofs, gutters and such,
They're very conscientious and they really do too much.

But Harry had an enemy a black-toothed kind of man,
They called him snotty Knotty and he drove the gaffer's van,
He tried to catch them dodging in his snidy kind of way,
And even stopped their bonus so they had very little pay,
Then one day while out sniding instead of watching where he was going,
Snotty crashed into the back of a wagon and that was his undoing.

Now Snotty is in Heaven in that grand old lodge above,
And Harry often wonders if he prayer had been the shove,
For now he makes good money, holidays abroad and all the rest,
So raise your glasses high my lads and say Harry all the best.

Harry Ord

INFORMATION

We hope you have enjoyed reading this book - and that you will continue to enjoy it in the coming years.

If you like reading and writing poetry drop us a line, or give us a call, and we'll send you a free information pack.

Write to

        Poetry Now Information
        1-2 Wainman Road
        Woodston
        Peterborough
        PE2 7BU